Boost Creative Writing pack

Planning Sheets to Support Writers (Especially SEN Pupils) in Years 1–6

Judith Thornby

CONTENTS
Boost Creative Writing, Years 1–2
Boost Creative Writing, Years 3–4
Boost Creative Writing, Years 5–6

We hope you and your pupils enjoy using the ideas in this book. Brilliant Publications publishes many other books to help primary school teachers. To find out more details on all of our titles, including those listed below, please go to our website: www.brilliantpublications.co.uk.

Brilliant Activities for Reading Comprehension, Year 1	978-1-78317-070-8
Brilliant Activities for Reading Comprehension, Year 2	978-1-78317-071-5
Brilliant Activities for Reading Comprehension, Year 3	978-1-78317-072-2
Brilliant Activities for Reading Comprehension, Year 4	978-1-78317-073-9
Brilliant Activities for Reading Comprehension, Year 5	978-1-78317-074-6
Brilliant Activities for Reading Comprehension, Year 6	978-1-78317-075-3
Brilliant Activities for Creative Writing, Year 1	978-0-85747-463-6
Brilliant Activities for Creative Writing, Year 2	978-0-85747-464-3
Brilliant Activities for Creative Writing, Year 3	978-0-85747-465-0
Brilliant Activities for Creative Writing, Year 4	978-0-85747-466-7
Brilliant Activities for Creative Writing, Year 5	978-0-85747-467-4
Brilliant Activities for Creative Writing, Year 6	978-0-85747-468-1
Developing Reading Comprehension Skills Years 5-6: Classic Children's Literature	978-0-85747-837-5
Developing Reading Comprehension Skills Years 5-6: Classic Poetry	978-0-85747-846-7
How to Achieve Outstanding Writers in the EYFS and KS1	978-0-85747-838-2
Cracking Creative Writing	978-0-85747-831-3
Boost Spelling Skills	978-0-85747-803-0

Published by Brilliant Publications Limited
Unit 10
Sparrow Hall Farm
Edlesborough
Dunstable
Bedfordshire
LU6 2ES, UK

www.brilliantpublications.co.uk

The name Brilliant Publications and the logo are registered trademarks.

Written by Judith Thornby
Illustrated by Cathy Hughes
Cover illustration by Frank Endersby
Designed by Brilliant Publications Limited

© Text Judith Thornby 2014
© Design Brilliant Publications Limited 2021

Printed book ISBN: 978-0-85747-931-0
E-book ISBN: 978-1-78317-107-1

First printed and published in the UK in 2021

The right of Judith Thornby to be identified as the author of this work has been asserted by herself in accordance with the Copyright, Designs and Patents Act 1988.

Pages displaying the note *'This page may be photocopied for use by the purchasing institution only.'* may be copied by individual teachers acting on behalf of the purchasing institution for classroom use only, without permission from the publisher and without declaration to the Copyright Licensing Agency or Publishers' Licensing Services. The materials may not be reproduced in any other form or for any other purpose without the prior permission of the publisher.

Ages: 5–7yrs

Boost Creative Writing
Planning Sheets to Support Writers (Especially SEN Pupils) in Years 1–2

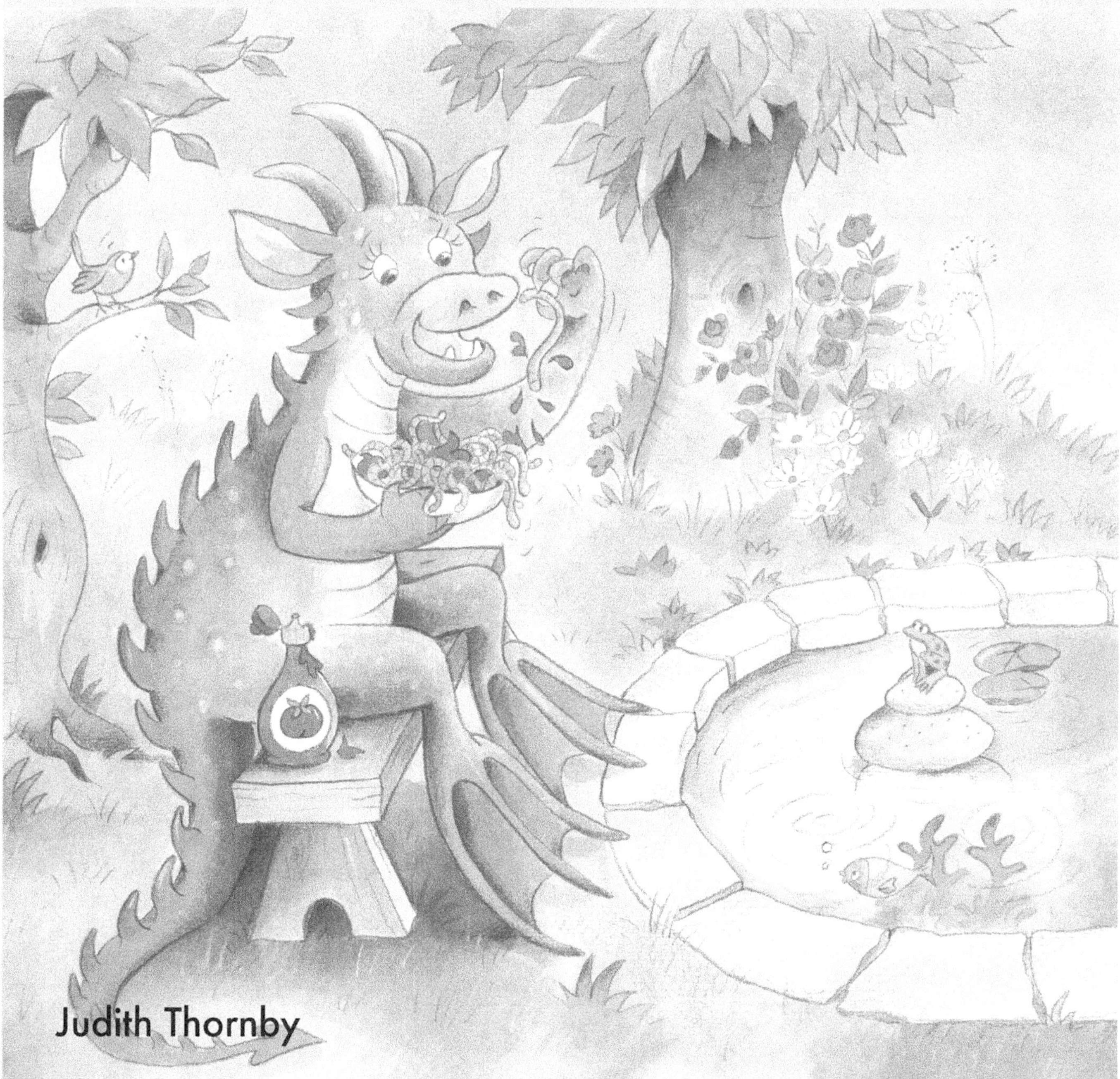

Judith Thornby

Boost Creative Writing

Planning Sheets to Support Writers (Especially SEN Pupils) in Years 1–2

Judith Thornby

We hope you and your pupils enjoy using the ideas in this book. Brilliant Publications publishes many other books to help primary school teachers. To find out more details on all of our titles, including those listed below, please go to our website: www.brilliantpublications.co.uk.

Boost Creative Writing – Years 3–4	978-1-78317-059-3
Boost Creative Writing – Years 5–6	978-1-78317-060-9
Brilliant Activities for Reading Comprehension, Year 1	978-1-78317-070-8
Brilliant Activities for Reading Comprehension, Year 2	978-1-78317-071-5
Brilliant Activities for Reading Comprehension, Year 3	978-1-78317-072-2
Brilliant Activities for Reading Comprehension, Year 4	978-1-78317-073-9
Brilliant Activities for Reading Comprehension, Year 5	978-1-78317-074-6
Brilliant Activities for Reading Comprehension, Year 6	978-1-78317-075-3
Brilliant Activities for Creative Writing, Year 1	978-0-85747-463-6
Brilliant Activities for Creative Writing, Year 2	978-0-85747-464-3
Brilliant Activities for Creative Writing, Year 3	978-0-85747-465-0
Brilliant Activities for Creative Writing, Year 4	978-0-85747-466-7
Brilliant Activities for Creative Writing, Year 5	978-0-85747-467-4
Brilliant Activities for Creative Writing, Year 6	978-0-85747-468-1
Developing Reading Comprehension Skills Years 5-6: Classic Children's Literature	978-0-85747-837-5
Developing Reading Comprehension Skills Years 5-6: Classic Poetry	978-0-85747-846-7
How to Achieve Outstanding Writers in the EYFS and KS1	978-0-85747-838-2
Cracking Creative Writing	978-0-85747-831-3
Boost Spelling Skills	978-0-85747-803-0

Published by Brilliant Publications Limited
Unit 10
Sparrow Hall Farm
Edlesborough
Dunstable
Bedfordshire
LU6 2ES, UK

www.brilliantpublications.co.uk

The name Brilliant Publications and the logo are registered trademarks.

Written by Judith Thornby
Illustrated by Cathy Hughes
Cover illustration by Frank Endersby
Designed by Brilliant Publications Limited

© Text Judith Thornby 2014
© Design Brilliant Publications Limited 2014

Printed book ISBN: 978-1-78317-058-6
E-book ISBN: 978-1-78317-061-6

First printed and published in the UK in 2014

The right of Judith Thornby to be identified as the author of this work has been asserted by herself in accordance with the Copyright, Designs and Patents Act 1988.

Pages 6–73 may be copied by individual teachers acting on behalf of the purchasing institution for classroom use only, without permission from the publisher and without declaration to the Copyright Licensing Agency or Publishers' Licensing Services. The materials may not be reproduced in any other form or for any other purpose without the prior permission of the publisher.

Contents

Introduction	4
Links to the National Curriculum	5
Suggested writing targets	6

Adventure story
Fifi and the beanstalk	7
Fifi and the snake	8
Fifi and the dog	9
Fifi and the pull-along dog	10
Sam and the Queen	11
Sam and the dragon egg	12
Sam and the cross crab	13
Freddie Frog	14
The Queen pops out	15–16
The magic carpet	17
Toto's adventure	18
The red balloon	19–21
Stuck on the island	22–23

Descriptive account
About me	24
My home	25
My dad	26
My mummy	27
My friend	28
Who am I?	29
My day as a Victorian child	30
My dream party	31
Autumn – I can see	32–33

Fairy tale
Create a fairy tale	34–35
Create a character for a fairy tale	36–37
Create a setting for a fairy tale	38–39

Fantasy
The super mini-beast	40
My pet monster	41–42
It's time to go out	43–44

Information report
Our trip to the seaside	45
Victorian seaside	46
The story of Grace Darling	47–48
The story of Emily Davison	49–50
The story of Rosa Parks	51–52
Christopher Columbus	54–54
The first man on the moon	55–56

Letter/Review
A letter to Santa	57–58
Book review	59
A review of Year 2	60

Poetry
Rain	61–62
My home	63
Grandad	64–65
Fireworks	66–67
Mini-beasts	68–69
Spring	70–71

Templates
Story mountain template	72
Mind map template	73

Introduction

These series of planning sheets aim to provide a structured resource which gives plenty of scope for exploring and collecting ideas in the different writing genres: adventure, fantasy, recount, letter, poetry etc. They generate discussion within a defined framework and then aid pupils to write more descriptive stories and compose longer pieces of writing.

Reluctant writers or those writers who struggle with the organization of their ideas can express themselves with more self-assurance by using these planning sheets. Confident writers can also benefit by delving into them to gain further ideas.

Some sheets can be written on directly but many are designed as a prop to refer to when writing. Vocabulary sheets are incorporated with some stories to help the flow of ideas.

Story mountain and mind map templates are included to assist narrative and descriptive writing and to cater for different learning styles. Visual learners have lots of imaginative ideas but might struggle with the sequence of events or the bare skeleton of the story so can benefit from using the story mountain approach. Logical systematic learners can sequence ideas but might struggle to develop them creatively and can benefit from using the mind map templates to expand descriptive writing.

I have specialized in the field of learning support since 1997 when I gained a diploma in specific learning difficulties. I am especially interested in promoting creative writing skills with children who are reluctant writers or who struggle with the organization of their ideas. These series of planning sheets generate discussion and aid in structuring composition in the different writing genres. They also can be used to give further ideas to confident writers as well. I have found that they have been successful in giving pupils greater self-assurance to express themselves in written form and have helped to make writing an enjoyable experience!

On page 5 you will see how the activities in the book link to the 2014 National Curriculum for England. On page 6 there are suggested writing targets. The way I use these is to cut out the relevant one(s) and tape them to the top of the sheets prior to copying, so that pupils have the targets in front of them as they work.

Links to the National Curriculum

The sheets in **Boost Creative Writing** will help Year 1 and 2 pupils to develop their composition skills, as set out in the National Curriculum for England (2014).

Year 1 – Composition

It is important for children to talk about what they are going to write prior to attempting to put their ideas on paper. The sheets in **Boost Creative Writing** are designed to do just that.

Through talking about what they want to write about, children can be encouraged to compose sentences orally and sequence their ideas to form short narratives. The adventure story sheets, in particular, encourage pupils to think about the structure of the story – what happens next? And then? What happens at the end?

After pupils have finished writing, encourage them to talk about what they have written with you or other pupils and to check that what they have written makes sense.

Reading their writing aloud helps children to see that their writing is valued. The poetry sheets are particularly good for this.

Year 2 – Composition

The sheets in **Boost Creative Writing** provide opportunities for pupils to write a range of different types of writing, from narratives and descriptive accounts, to information reports on real events and poetry. They will not only learn how to write for different purposes, they will also develop stamina for writing. Some of the information reports link to the History Programme of Study.

The sheets are designed to encourage children to talk about what they are going to write prior to doing so. The sheets provide opportunities for children to jot down ideas and key words. Many of the sheets have ideas and vocabulary that will act as prompts to stimulate pupils to discuss, prior to writing, what they want to say and how best to say it.

The design of the sheets, with boxes for each sentence or key idea, will aid children in putting their thoughts in order and help them to structure their writing in a logical way.

Pupils should be encouraged to re-read their work and make simple additions, revisions and corrections. Reading their writing aloud, to a teacher or other pupils, is a particularly valuable way of helping pupils to notice where and how their writing could be improved. In addition to checking for errors in spelling, grammar and punctuation, they should also be encouraged to check consistency of verb tenses.

As with Year 1, pupils should be encouraged to read their work aloud, with appropriate intonation.

Vocabulary, grammar and punctuation

Many of the sheets contain suggested vocabulary to encourage children to extend their range of vocabulary and prompt them to use new words in their writing. All the activities can also be used to reinforce children's understanding of grammar and punctuation, but this is not the primary purpose of the sheets.

Suggested writing targets

	Relates to
To remember to start a sentence with a capital letter	Any
To put a full stop at the end of every sentence	Any
To use full sentences in my writing	Any
To use capital letters and full stops in my story	Any story
To leave finger spaces between words	Any
To use 3 WOW words in my story	Any story
To use the words 'one day', 'then' and 'finally' in my story	Any story
To start some of my sentences with these words: Then… After that… Suddenly… Next minute… Finally…	Any story
To link sentences using the word 'because' in my writing	Any
To link sentences using some of these words in my writing: 'because', 'but', 'and', 'so', 'until'	Any
To use different words for 'ran' in 'Toto's adventure' story: hopped, jumped, scuttled, scampered, scurried	Toto's adventure
To use adjectives in my writing	Any
To start my story with an interesting sentence	Any story
To write a story with a beginning, middle and an ending	Any story
To plan my character description by drawing a picture and adding adjectives before writing	Fairy tale My pet monster
To write a magical fairytale, thinking about setting and character	Fairy tale
To describe myself as well as possible using WOW words	About me Who am I?
To use 5 WOW words in a detailed description of a pet monster	My pet monster
To play around with NOISY words and make up a firework poem	Fireworks
To start each line of my poem with a capital letter	Any poem
To use rhyming words in my 'Rain' poem	Rain
To use these words in a poem about a mini-beast: Next to… Under… Beside… In… On… Near…	Mini-beasts
To write 4–5 super sentences in my description of autumn	Autumn – I can see
To write a book review, including a short description of the main character and plot as well as my view of the book	Book review

Fifi and the beanstalk

One day
What does Fifi do?

| plants a bean shoot | sun shines | rain falls | gets bigger |

Then
What does Fifi do?

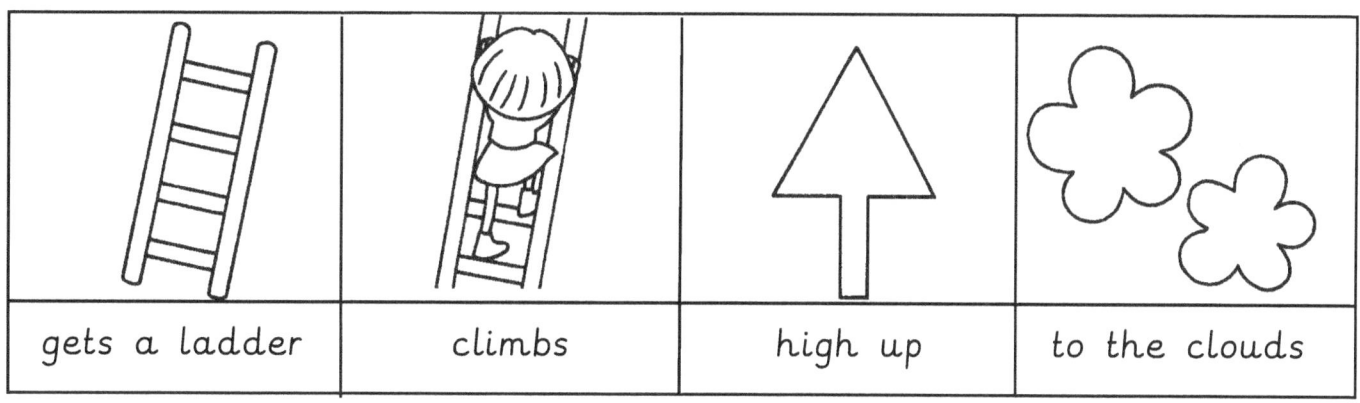

| gets a ladder | climbs | high up | to the clouds |

After that
What does Fifi find? What is it full of?

| magic basket | full of | climbs down |

Finally
What happens at the end?

Fifi and the snake

One day
What does Fifi do?

| wakes up | sunny day | puts on her skates |

Then
What happens?

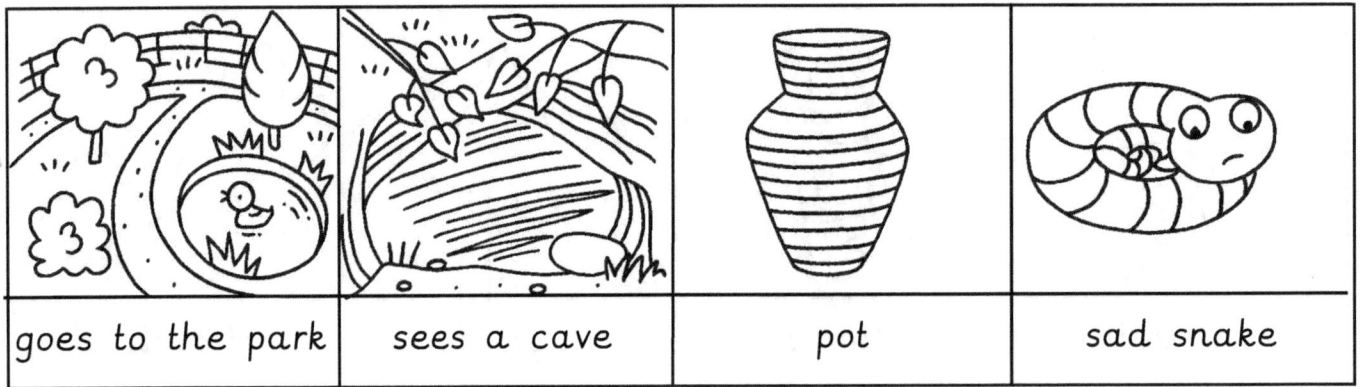

| goes to the park | sees a cave | pot | sad snake |

After that
What does Fifi do?

| gives it | a cake | to eat |

Finally
What happens at the end?

Fifi and the dog

Adventure story

One day
What does Fifi do?

| goes to the park | plays with her teddy bear | kicks the ball | water |

Then
What happens?

| dog | runs into water | gets wet | Fifi says |

After that
What happens next?

Finally
What happens at the end?

Useful words
the   with   it   and   they   she   into   go   home

Boost Creative Writing, Years 1–2
© Judith Thornby and Brilliant Publications Limited

Fifi and the pull-along dog

One day
What does Fifi do?

| wakes up | gets her toy dog | pulls it outside |

Then
What happens?

| sees a door | pushes it open | stops at a tree |

After that
What does Fifi do?

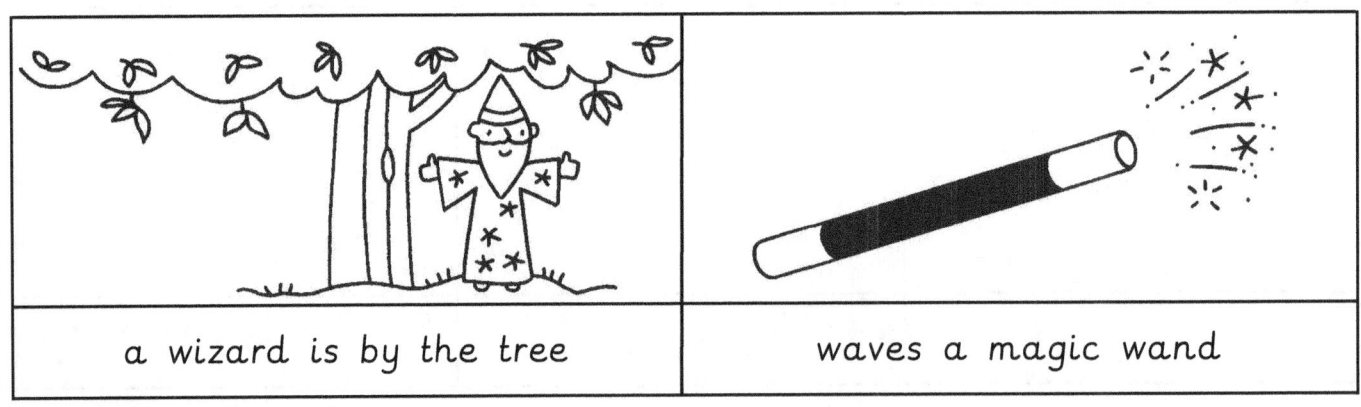

| a wizard is by the tree | waves a magic wand |

Finally
Fifi's pull-along dog becomes real!

Sam and the Queen

One day
What does Sam do?

Then
What does Sam do?

After that
What happens next?

Finally
What happens at the end?

Sam and the dragon egg

One day
What does Sam do?

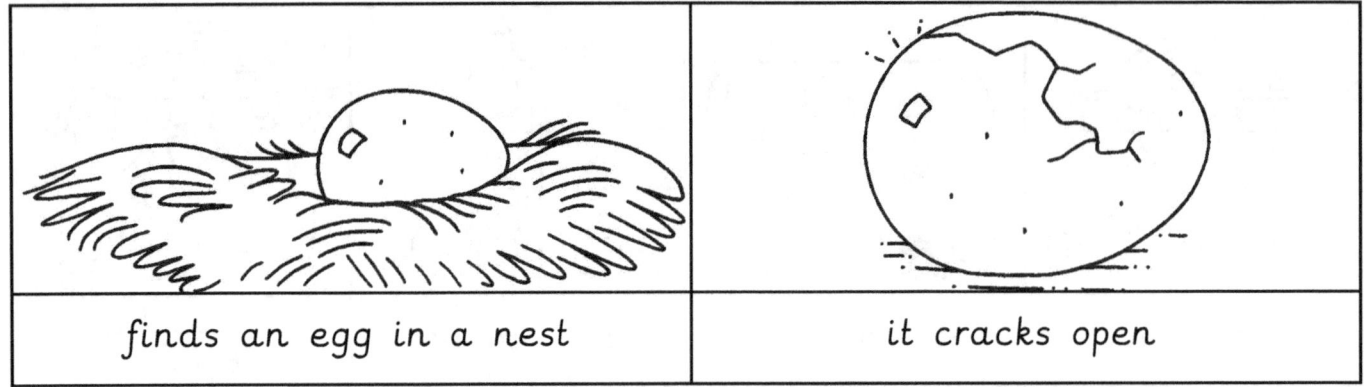

| finds an egg in a nest | it cracks open |

Then
What happens?

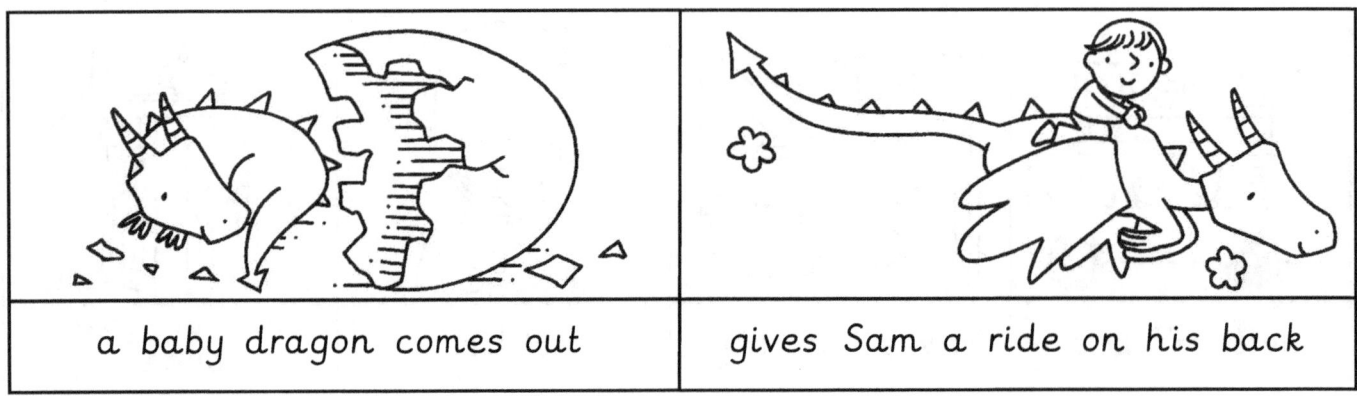

| a baby dragon comes out | gives Sam a ride on his back |

After that
What happens next?

Where shall we go?

| Where do they go? | What do they see? |

Finally
What happens at the end?

Sam and the cross crab

One day
What does Sam do?

| gets his spade | digs in the sand | finds a crab |

Then
What does he do?

| puts it in a bucket | |

After that
Then what happens?

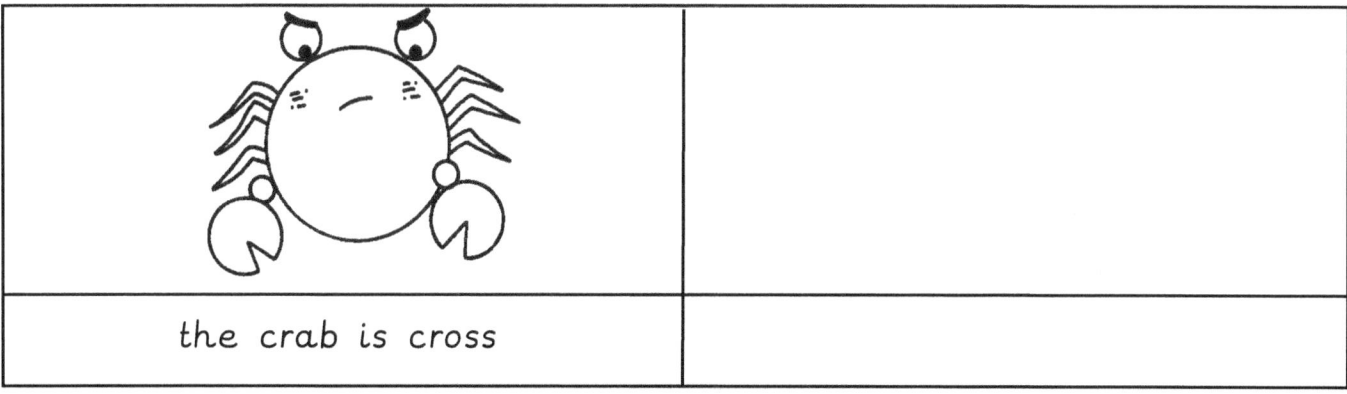

| the crab is cross | |

Finally
What happens at the end?

Freddie Frog

One day
What does Freddie Frog do?

| hops into a garden | sees a wheelbarrow |

Then
What happens?

| hops into a greenhouse | sees a bee |

After that
What does Freddie do?

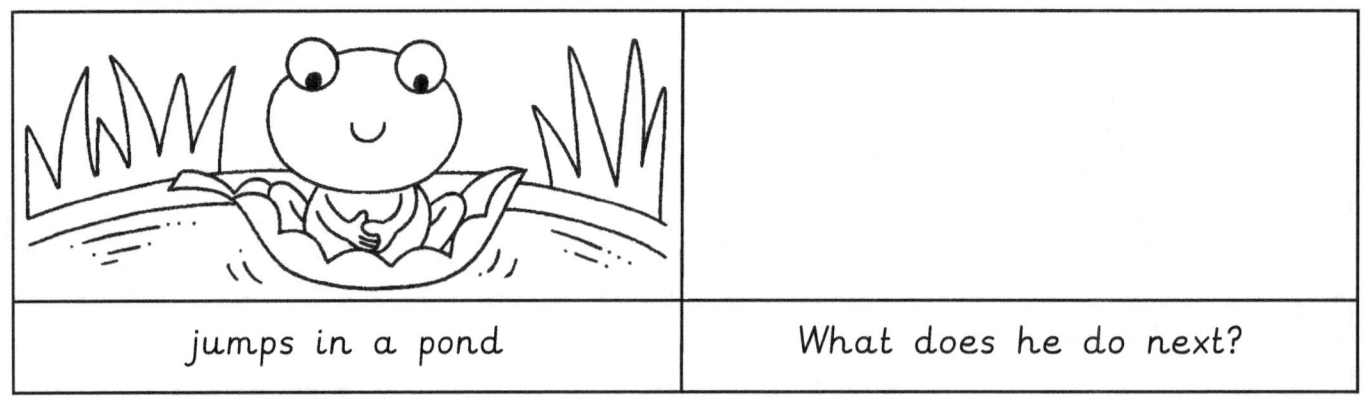

| jumps in a pond | What does he do next? |

Finally
What happens in the end?

The Queen pops out

One day
The Queen pops out of the palace in disguise.

| she puts on an old... | she dyes her hair... | she will not wear her... | she will not take her... |

Then
What happens?

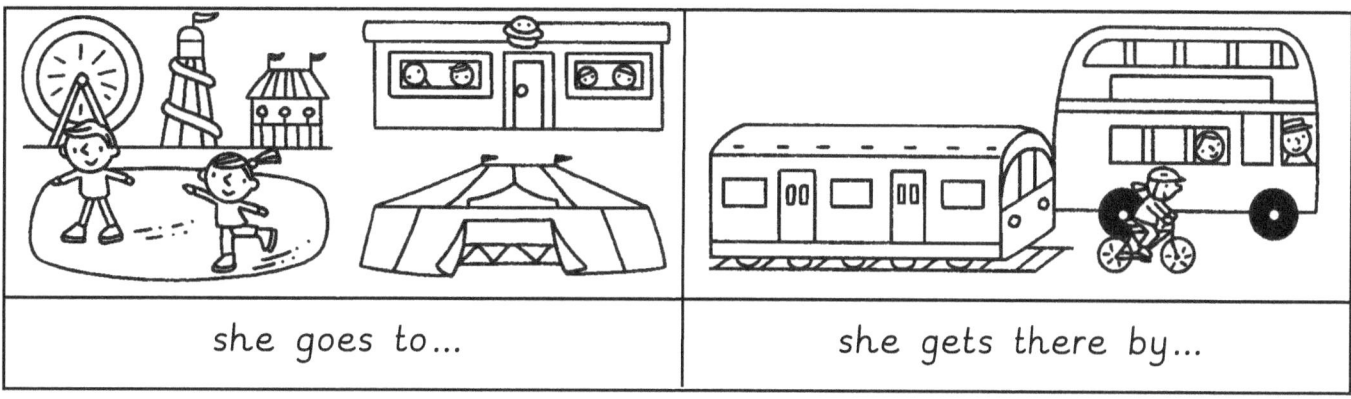

| she goes to... | she gets there by... |

After that
What happens?

| while she is there she... | and then she... |

Finally
She goes back to the palace. She has had a _____ time.

Will she go out in disguise again?

The Queen pops out

Use some of these words to help you write your story.

hair
red
black
brown
dress coat
wig
pair of
  sunglasses

crown jewels
carriage
corgis

bus
walks
rides on a bicycle
train
underground

shopping centre
ice rink
zoo
circus
McDonalds
fun fair

buys a hat
skates round the rink
sees an elephant
eats a burger
has a ride on the dodgems

fantastic
great day
good fun

The magic carpet

Write a story about someone who found a magic carpet and could go for a ride on it anywhere in the world.

Who?
Where did the person find the carpet?
What did it look like?

Ideas: in the attic   in a shop   at the back of an old wardrobe

What happened next? Then?
What could the person see?

Ideas: floated up in the air   zoomed   whizzed

Where did the magic carpet take the person?

Ideas: amusement park   seaside   the moon

Write about two or more things that happened there.
What did the person bring home?

Finally
What happened to the carpet?
Was it ever used again?
What did the person think about the trip?

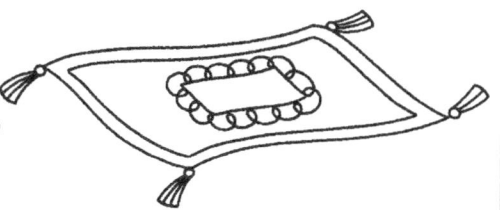

Toto's adventure

When Toto, the big white school rabbit, woke up, he noticed that his hutch door had not been shut properly. He ran off to see what was going on.

He hopped into the school garden.
What did he see? What did he hear?

After that?
He scampered into...

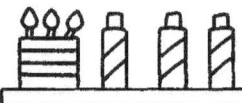 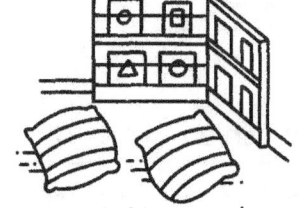 

Ideas: the store cupboard   reception class   school office

Who did he meet?
What did he see? How did he feel?

What did he smell coming from the kitchen?
Did he eat something?

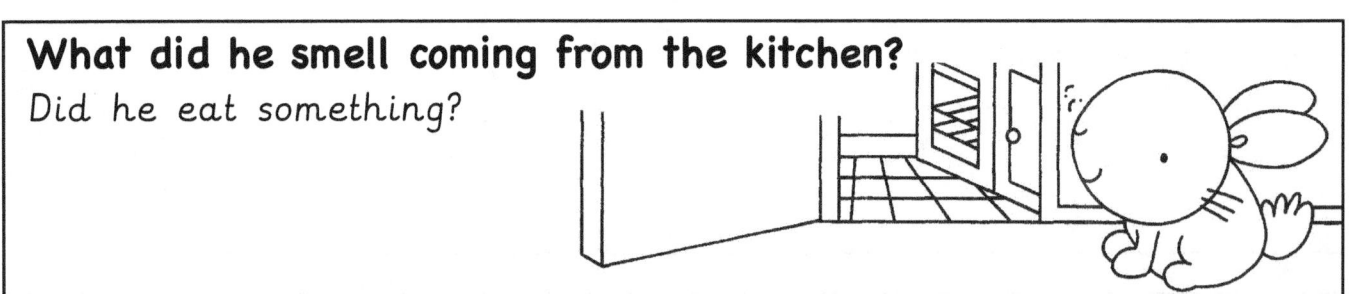

Finally
Toto went back to his hutch because...

Would Toto like to have another adventure?

The red balloon

Bobby, the big red balloon, floated high up into the sky. He floated into _____'s garden.
(your name)

What could Bobby see and hear in your garden?
He could see...   He could also see...
He could hear...

Ideas: trampoline   swing   cat   dog   bee   friend   brother

Then he floated to _____
(where you live)

What could he see and hear in your town/village?
He could see...
He could hear...

Ideas: bus   train station   baker's shop   postbox   fair

Then he floated to _____
(your school)

What could he see and hear?
He could see...
He could hear...

Ideas: playground   teacher   slide   pond   caretaker

Finally
What happened to Bobby the balloon?

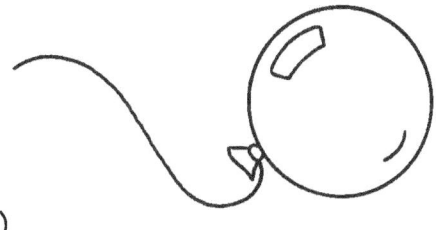

Ideas: popped   landed safely (where?)

The red balloon

Draw, colour and label a mind map of ideas.

What could it see?  hear?   smell?

In my garden

In my town/village

At school

The red balloon

Read this story to generate some ideas.

> One day Bobby the red balloon floats high up into the air. There is a fluffy cloud in the blue sky. He hears an aeroplane pass by. He looks down into Yassin's garden. He hears a busy bee buzzing in the garden. It is getting some nectar from a flower so it can make some honey. He can see a washing line and there are two red socks and a blue shirt on the line. He sees Yassin, who is nine years old, kicking a football. Yassin's dog, Rocky is chasing a little black cat into the house. Then he floats across to Anytown. He hears a train roaring into the station. He can see a cake shop and he smells some delicious chocolate cookies that have just come out of the oven. He drifts across to Any School. He can hear lots of children laughing in the playground. A girl called Molly is sliding down a slide. Then a teacher called Mrs McCooke blows the whistle and Molly has to line up with her class. Finally Bobby balloon floats down to the ground. He lands on a prickly leaf and suddenly he goes POP!

Further suggestions

◆ Use props – a balloon (helium if possible) and pictures as prompts to oral retelling of the story. Possible pictures: cloud, aeroplane, bee, washing line, dog, football, train, chocolate cookies, slide, whistle, holly).

◆ Make sure that pupils are using full sentences when orally recounting each part of the story.

◆ Emphasize using words 'Then…', After that…', 'Suddenly…', 'Finally…'

◆ Pupils to draw pictures for their own stories (help them to label with descriptive words as required) and ensure pupils use these pictorial sheets as an aid when writing.

Stuck on the island

Write a story about two children who have rowed their boat to an island and got stuck on it when the boat disappeared.

It was a beautiful sunny day and the sea was very calm – just the sort of day to visit the island.

Who are the children?
How do they get across to the island?

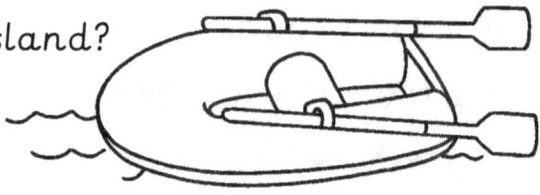

Write about three things they did when they got to the island.

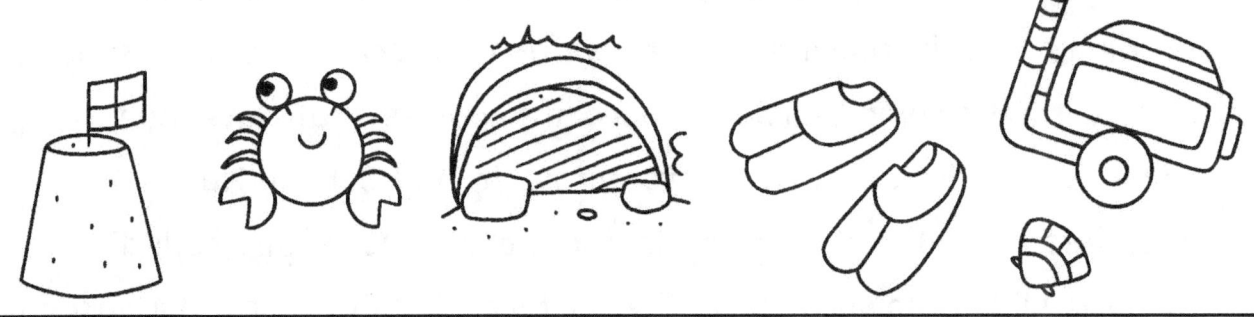

What did they have for their picnic lunch?

    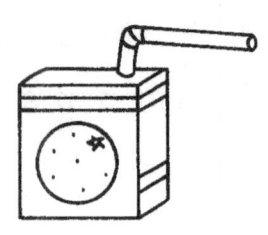

What did they do when they discovered their boat had gone?
How did they feel?
What happened next?
Who came to their rescue?

Finally
When they were back home, their mum said...

Stuck on the island

 Adventure story

Use some of these words to help you write your story.

---

packed a picnic
rowed the boat to the island

---

built a sandcastle	went for a swim
rock pools	explored
caught a big crab	found a cave

---

sat down for lunch

sandwiches	apple
ham	banana
cheese	biscuit
crisps	cake
juice	orange squash

---

wanted to go home	heard noise
noticed	sound of
boat disappeared	lifeboat
looked everywhere	helicopter
upset	dolphin
felt worried	happy
	relieved
	rescued

After a while…
Next minute…
Suddenly…
Eventually…
Then…
At last…

About me

I am _____ years old.

I have _____ sister(s) and _____ brother(s).

0 1 2 3 4 5 6 7 8 9

This is my drawing of me.

I have

Ideas: rabbit(s)   fish   cat(s)   dog(s)

I like to

My home

I live in a _____ .

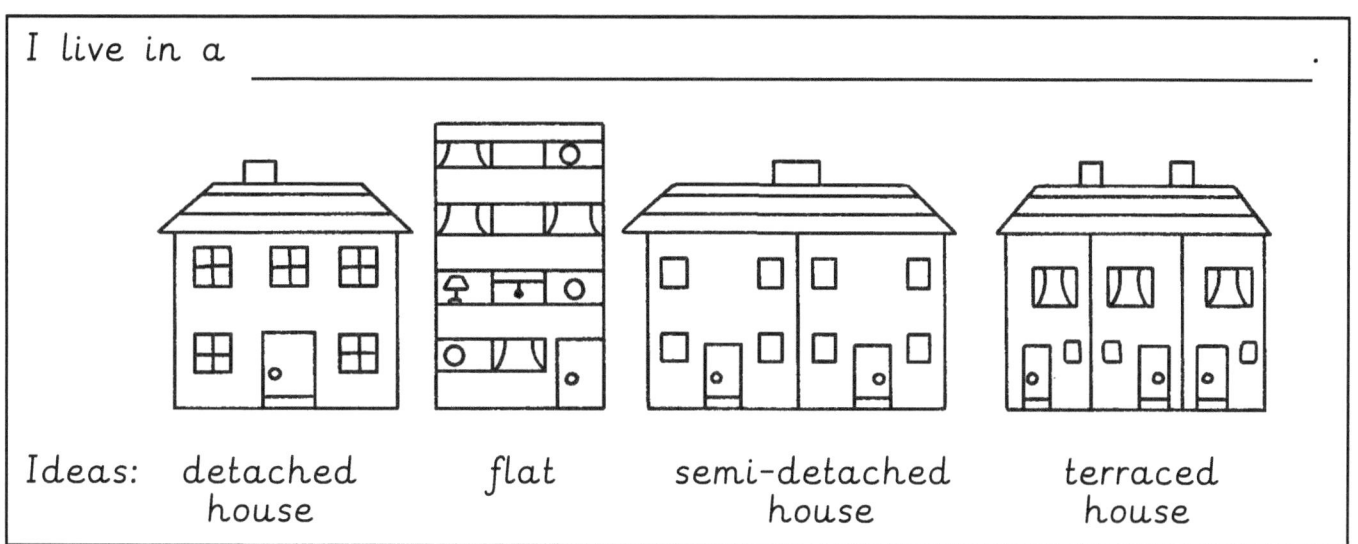

Ideas: detached house | flat | semi-detached house | terraced house

It has _____ bedrooms.

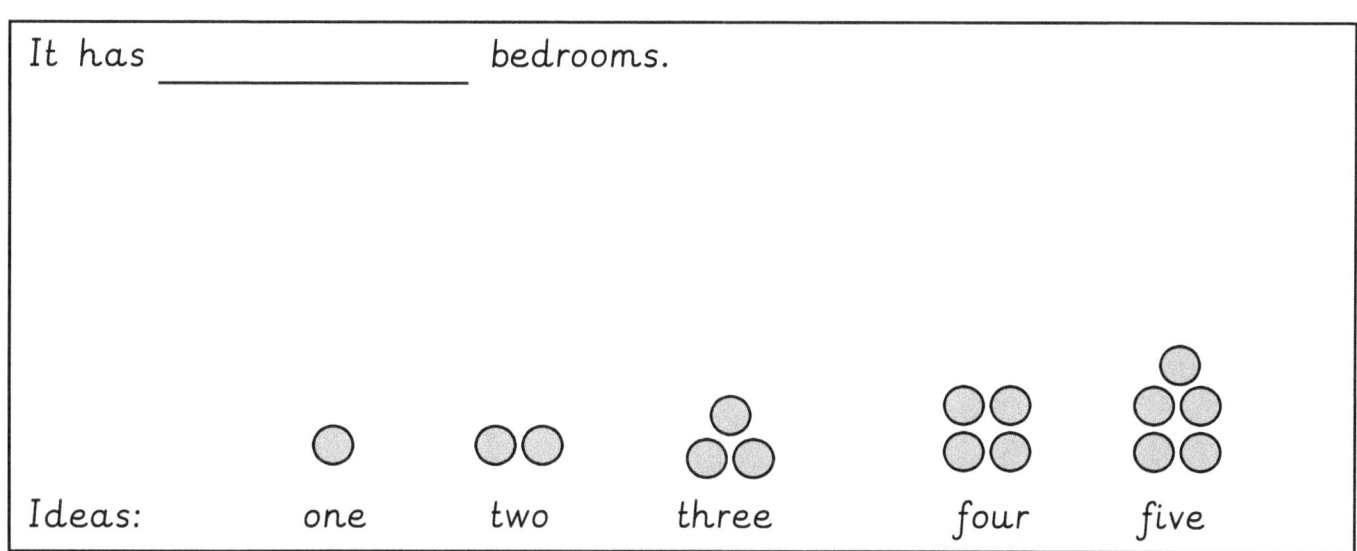

Ideas: one | two | three | four | five

My home has got a

Ideas:
garage   garden
chimney   extension
study   kitchen

This is my drawing of where I live.

Boost Creative Writing, Years 1–2
© Judith Thornby and Brilliant Publications Limited

This page may be photocopied for use by the purchasing institution only.

My dad

This is my drawing of my dad.

My dad has _____ brother(s) and _____ sister(s).

Ideas: no   one   two   three   four

My dad likes to

and

play football

read a paper

bake a cake

cut the grass

My mummy

This is my drawing of my mummy.

My mummy has _____ hair.

Ideas:
brown   black   blonde
ginger   long   short

My mummy likes to

and

read a book

walk the dog

sing a song

ride a bike

Boost Creative Writing, Years 1–2
© Judith Thornby and Brilliant Publications Limited

My friend

My friend has

hair   brown   black   blonde   ginger

long   short   curly   straight   bunches

eyes   blue   brown   grey

My friend

wears glasses   has freckles

My friend has

brother(s)?   sister(s)?   how old?

pets?   dog?   cat?   goldfish?   rabbit?

My friend is good at   **My friend likes**

drawing   PE   doing sums   playing football

I like my friend because

makes up... games to play
chooses... to be my partner
listens... to my secrets
invites me... for a play date
shares...   sweets

Who am I?

What do I look like?

hair brown   black   blonde   ginger

long   short   straight   curly   bunches

eyes blue   brown   grey

glasses   freckles   rosy cheeks

Who is in my family?

brother(s)?   sister(s)?   how old?

What pets do I have?

rabbit?   goldfish?   cat?   dog?

Where do I live?

What are my favourite things?

favourite food?   toy?   book?   film?

What am I good at?
What is the most exciting thing that I have done?
Is there anything I am not so keen on?

This year I am most looking forward to

My day as a Victorian child

I will put on

 a bonnet
 a flat cap
 a long dress
 my boots

At school I will

 write on a slate
 look at a blackboard
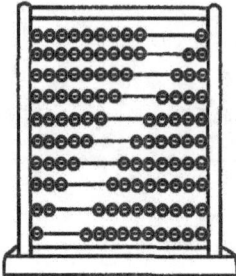 use an abacus
 be scared of the cane

Then I will play with

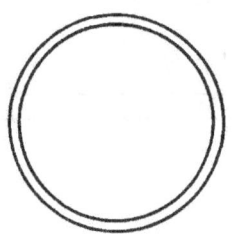 a hoop
 a hobby horse
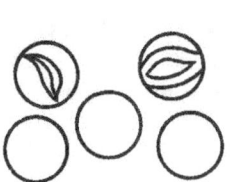 marbles
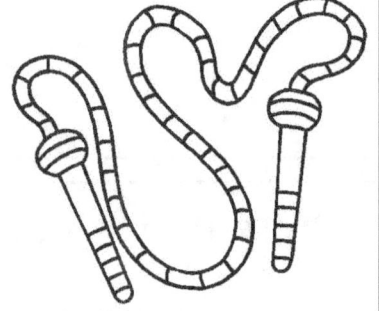 skipping rope

After that I will

 use a washboard to wash my clothes
 put a warming pan in my bed
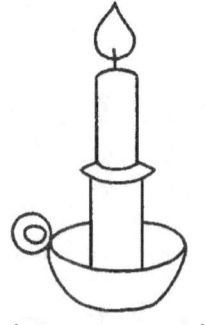 light a candle

My dream party

Where will you go? How? What will you do?

Deep under the sea

dolphin palace   swim with mermaid
collect shells   stare at the fish   eat shark cake

On the moon

rocket   hot air balloon   paint a star
dance with an alien   eat moon cookies

In nursery rhyme land

paint a rainbow   unicorn   sit on Humpty's   run after a
                                      wall   gingerbread man

It will be...

I will go with...

We will get there on a...

Then we will...

At teatime I will eat...

Finally I will...

Autumn – I can see

Collect leaves, conkers and other things you find in the autumn.

I can see

Autumn – I can see

Possible WOW words

brown yellow crispy dry	leaves	floating fluttering like kites dancing like ballerinas swirling like a snowstorm rustling crunching under my foot
juicy shiny spiky rosy smooth fat	berries conkers apples acorns pumpkins	growing waiting
busy sleepy/drowsy/dormant	squirrels flocks of... hedgehogs	looking for flying sleeping
sparkling wet	frost dew	lying

Create a fairy tale

Start: Once upon a time...
Setting
Characters: good, bad/naughty
Some trouble caused by bad character
Good character saves the day
End: they all live happily ever after

Setting

Ideas:
dark gloomy cave   beautiful castle/palace
cottage in the wood   deep under the sea

Characters

Ideas:
happy pixie   beautiful princess   sad giant
generous fairy   kind mermaid   handsome prince
bad dragon   wicked witch   naughty elf
sea monster

Story
What happens to the good person?

Ideas: is put under a spell   loses something special
gets captured   gets lost
Who helps? How?   has a trick played on him/her

What happens in the end?
(How is it all sorted?)
They all live happily ever after

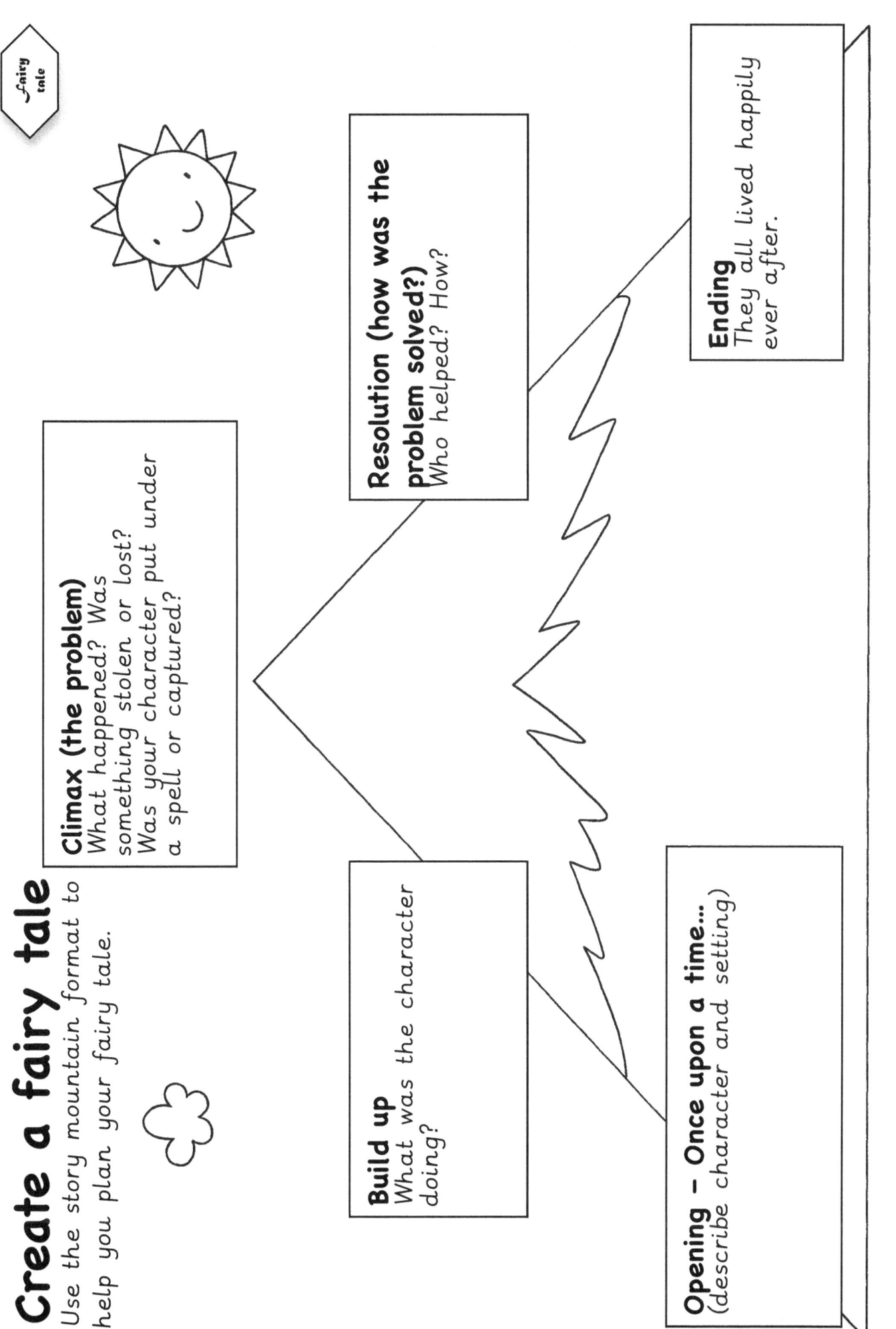

 fairy tale

Create a character for a fairy tale

Draw and colour a picture and then write about the character.

Who?

Ideas:
elf   mermaid   wizard   fairy   witch
princess   giant   sea monster   dragon   prince

What does your character look like?
Ideas:
size:	tall	short	plump	tiny	little
hair	eyes	ears	body	tail	wings
crown	shoes	wand	dress	pretty	beautiful
straight	curly	long	short	blonde	black
blue	silver	golden	scaly	pointed	sparkling

How does your character behave?

Ideas:
friendly   naughty   gentle   generous   kind hearted   untidy
funny   forgetful   greedy   lonely   wicked   shy

What does your character like doing?

Ideas:
making spells, playing tricks, collecting shells, combing her hair

Fairy tale character template

Create a character for a fairy tale.

My character is _____ .

Create a setting for a fairy tale

Draw and colour a picture and then write about the setting.

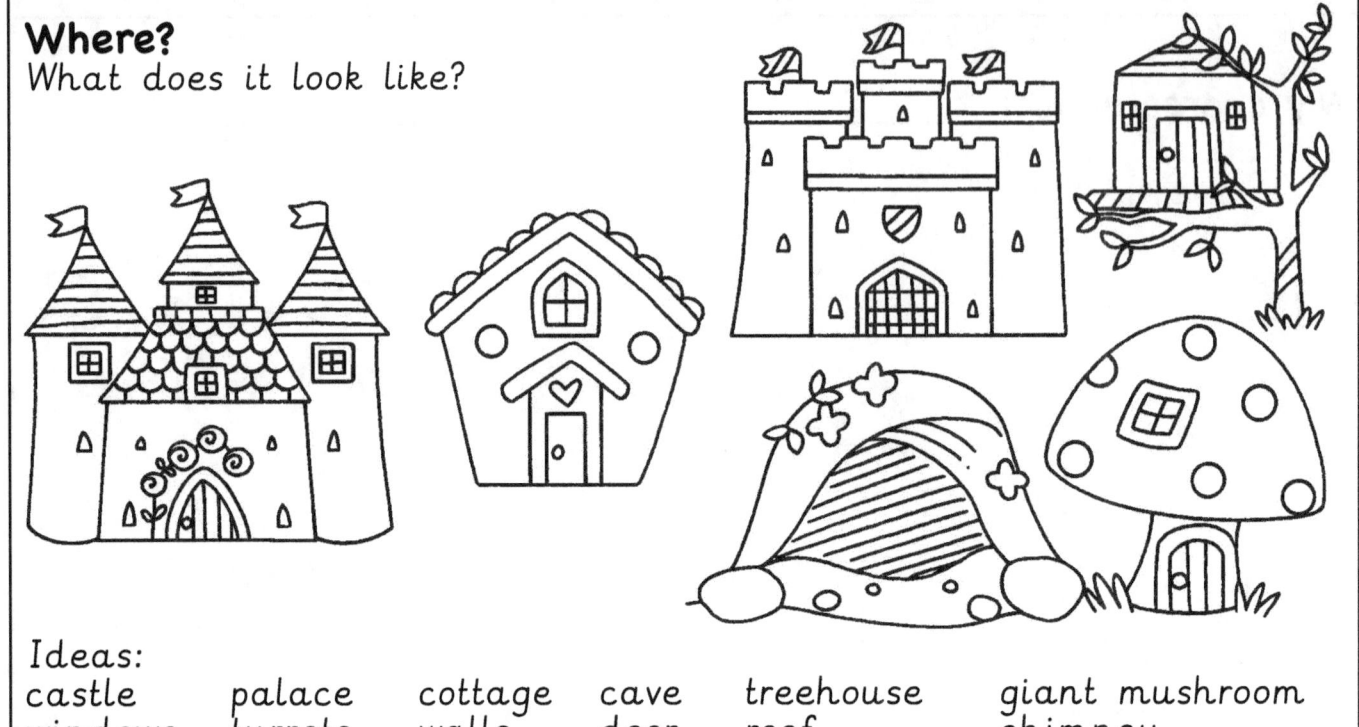

Where?
What does it look like?

Ideas:
castle   palace   cottage   cave   treehouse   giant mushroom
windows   turrets   walls   door   roof   chimney

Where is it?

Ideas:
on top of a hill   in a wood   in a forest
on an island   deep under the sea

What is near it?

Ideas:
lake   moat   fountain   garden   tall trees   little path
garden   flowers   fruit bushes   hedge   high wall   mountain
hill   shells   shipwreck   lobster pot   coral reef

This page may be photocopied for use by the purchasing institution only.

Boost Creative Writing, Years 1–2
© Judith Thornby and Brilliant Publications Limited

Fairy tale setting template

Create a setting for a fairy tale.

My setting is _____ .

 # The super mini-beast

Draw and colour a picture of a marvellous mini-beast.

Add labels

| wings | legs | body | antennae | spotty | hairy |
| striped | short | long | yellow | blue | orange |

What does it like to do?

Ideas:
flies   slithers   eats   collects   looks for   rests   wriggles

This page may be photocopied for use by the purchasing institution only.

Boost Creative Writing, Years 1–2
© Judith Thornby and Brilliant Publications Limited

My pet monster

Draw, colour and label a picture of your monster.

Name of monster:

_____

Use WOW words

Ideas:					
body	eyes	snout	fangs	tentacles
antennae	legs	webbed feet	claws	horn
scales	wings	tail	hairy	spotted
striped	spiky	pointed	smooth	

Boost Creative Writing, Years 1–2
© Judith Thornby and Brilliant Publications Limited

My pet monster

My monster is called _____.

What does your monster look like?

Ideas:
size?	shape?	colour?		
eyes	eyelashes	ears	body	snout
fangs	tentacles	wings	horn	tail
scales	fur	webbed feet		

Where does he sleep?
What's his bed like? What type of covers does his bed have?

Ideas:
in the attic
inside the shed
under a bush in the garden

What is his character like?
What does he do if he is happy? What does he do if he is angry?

Ideas:
shy   friendly   nervous   easy-going   turns invisible
glows   makes a noise like...

What do you feed him? How much?
Be imaginative!

Ideas:
... four fat juicy worms from the garden, covered in ketchup

How long have you had him? Why is he special?

Ideas:
helps me with my homework
plays games with me

It's time to go out

Write a story about a tiny person who went to see his or her friend in a very odd way. Be imaginative!

What time was it?

It was...

in the middle of the night   early in the morning

Who?

How does he/she travel? Where is the transport found?

Write about three amazing things seen on the way.

Ideas:
Who?   What was it doing?   Then what happened?

Idea number 1:
... passed a cloud and saw a spotted green bird. He was chasing a black cat. The cat had stolen an egg from his nest.

What happened when the person got to his/her friend's house?

Boost Creative Writing, Years 1–2
© Judith Thornby and Brilliant Publications Limited

 # It's time to go out

Draw, colour and label a mind map of your ideas. Be imaginative.

When does the tiny person travel? How? Where does he/she find the transport?

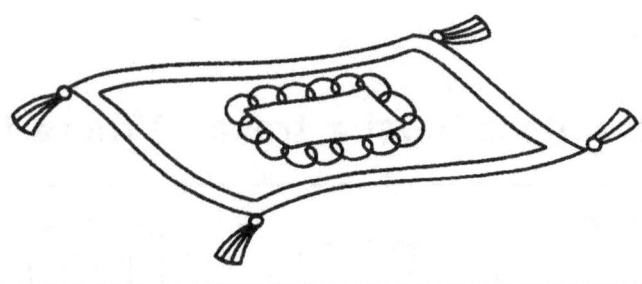

What three amazing things does he/she see on the way?

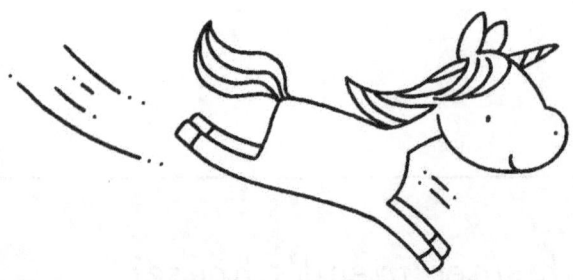

Our trip to the seaside

We went on a trip to the seaside.

First
How did we get there?

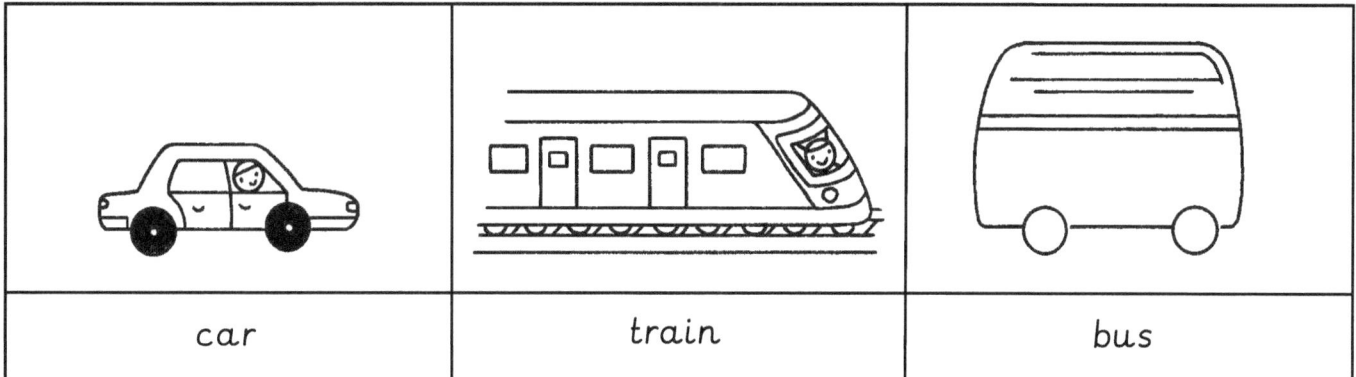

Then
What did we do?

After that
What did we eat?

Finally
What happened at the end? How did we get home?

Victorian seaside

Bessie and Albert went to the seaside.

First
What did they do first?

| made a sandcastle | changed in a bathing hut | paddled in the sea |

Then
What did they do?

| had a donkey ride | saw a Punch and Judy show | ate an ice cream |

After that
What did they do?

| went to the pier | penny slot machines | heard the band playing |

Finally
What happened at the end? How did they get home?
Idea: Did they go by steam train?

The story of Grace Darling

Write about the story of brave Grace Darling who helped her father one stormy night in 1838.

Who was Grace Darling?
Where did she live?

What happened one night?
What did she see that worried her?

What happened next?
How did she help?

Describe the rescue
Ideas:

clinging to rocks   blankets   cold and tired

What happened afterwards?

The story of Grace Darling

Use some of these words to help you write your report.

Who was Grace Darling?
lived
Farne
father
island
Longstone
lighthouse
busy
helped
strong
rower

What happened one night?
7th September 1838	wrecked	early one morning
sinking	terrible storm	large hole in the ship
ship	people clinging to	slippery rocks
trouble	drowning	

What happened next? Describe the rescue
saw danger	scared
begged father	fingers blue with cold
rowing boat	rescued
swamped by waves	nine people still alive
storm raged	made two trips

What happened afterwards?
survivors
safe
exhausted
looked after
so grateful
medal
bravery
risked her own life

Useful connecting words
After a while
Suddenly
Then
Meanwhile
Eventually
At last

The story of Emily Davison

Write about Emily Davison, a 'lawless lassie', who wanted women to be able to vote.

Who was Emily Davison?
(Was she a suffragette?)

Emily Davison was born in 1872.

She was...

What did she want women to have?
(Did she break the law to get attention?)

Emily Davison wanted women over 21 to have a...

She got into trouble because...

One day
(What did Emily do at Epsom Racecourse? Did she do it to get publicity?)

Emily ducked under the barrier on the race course track and...

Then...? After that?
(What happened to Emily at Epsom Racecourse? Did the horse trample her?)

Finally
(Was the law changed?)

The law was changed in...

Boost Creative Writing, Years 1–2
© Judith Thornby and Brilliant Publications Limited

The story of Emily Davison

Use some of this information to help you write your story.

born in London in
   October 1872
very bright student
took classes at
   university but wasn't
   allowed to get a
   degree as she was a
   woman
worked as a governess
   and a teacher

thought all people should be equal
wanted votes for women
joined suffragettes
unlawful acts to attract publicity
given nickname 'the lawless lassie'
went to prison many times

38 years old in 1913
Derby Day
ducked under barrier at Epsom Racecourse
grabbed bridle of King George V's horse
tried to pin 'Votes for women' sash on the horse
horse trampled her
died four days later in hospital

In 1928 all women over 21 allowed to vote

The story of Rosa Parks

Write about Rosa Parks who, on one day in 1955, refused to be treated unfairly any longer.

Who was Rosa Parks?
Where did she live?

Rosa Parks was born in 1913.

She lived in…

What was the law on the buses in the 'deep south' of United States up to 1956?

The law up to 1956 on the buses was…

One day
(Why was Rosa Parks on the bus? What did she do?)

Rosa refused to…

Then… After that…
She was taken to _____ for the night.

(Did African Americans refuse to use the buses in support?)

Finally
(Did the bus company lose money?)

The law was changed in…

The story of Rosa Parks

Use some of these words to help you write your story.

born in 1913
lived in Alabama in 'deep south' of United States
African American (black)
worked as a seamstress

special law – Jim Crow law – made it legal to discriminate against black people
segregation
seats on bus reserved for white people
if not enough seats for white people, black people had to give up their seats

long day at work
very tired
riding home on bus
no seats for a white person
spent night in jail
expected to give up her seat

did not think it fair
refused
broke the law
arrested
had to pay fine

in support of Rosa Parks
across country
many African Americans
formed civil rights group
wanted everyone to be treated fairly
led by Martin Luther King
refused to use buses until law was changed
bus company lost money
law finally changed in 1956
Rosa became a national hero

Christopher Columbus

Write about Christopher Columbus who discovered a 'new world'.

Who was Christopher Columbus?
He was born in 1451.
He lived in...
He went to sea when he was...

Where did he want to travel? Why?
He wanted to travel to...

(Did Queen Isabella of Spain give him the money to travel?)

One day
He was in command of three ships called...

They set sail and discovered...
(Where did he think he had gone?)
He thought he had sailed to...

Then
(How many voyages did he make to the 'new world'?)

He made _____ voyages.

Finally
(Why is he remembered?)

Christopher Columbus is remembered because...

Christopher Columbus

Use some of these words to help you write your report.

born in 1451
lived in Italy and Portugal
sailor – went to sea as a teenager
great explorer

wanted to sail to India, China and Japan
rich in gold, spices and jewels
Queen Isabella of Spain gave him money
not easy – few maps

sailed west
command of three ships: the Pinta, the Niña and the Santa María
landed in America
discovered the Caribbean islands of Jamaica and Trinidad
New World
called people 'Indians'
thought he had landed in India
claimed land for Spain
made four voyages altogether

died in 1506
remembered as a skilled sailor and navigator
first European person to visit new lands
people in Europe started to travel to North and South America

The first man on the moon

Write about Neil Armstrong who ws the first man ever to step on the moon.

Who was Neil Armstrong?
(When was he born? Where did he live? What was his job?)

Neil was born in...

He became an...

His spaceship was called...

One day in 1969
(What did he do? Where was he going? How long did it take?)

He was going to...

It took him ____ days to reach the moon.

Then he got into the lunar module
(What was the surface of the moon like?)

It was difficult to land on the moon because...

On the moon
He collected...

Finally he left the moon
(When did he get back to earth? Are his footsteps still visible on the moon? Why?)

The first man on the moon

Use some of these words to help you write your report.

Neil Armstrong
born in 1930
lived in Ohio in America
always wanted to be a pilot
flew over 200 types of aircraft
passed difficult tests
became an astronaut
captain of Apollo 11 spaceship
wanted the challenge of going to moon

blasted off from Kennedy space centre in Florida
July 1969
three day journey to the moon
boarded lunar module (Eagle) to get down to the moon

landed safely
difficult landing
had to avoid huge boulders, some the size of small cars
climbed out of module
'that's one small step for man, one giant leap for mankind'
on moon for 21 hours
nearly ran out of fuel
collected moon rocks

mission went well
3 days later module landed in Pacific Ocean

national hero
America had won the race to put the first man ever on moon
footprints still on moon – thick dust no wind

A letter to Santa

Dear Santa,

I have been good because I

| helped | tidied | worked hard at school |

I would like

| football | bike | crayons |
| construction set | doll | game |

I have left you a _____ and

_____ for the reindeer.

| drink | carrots | cookie | apple |

Love from,

Letter/ Review

A letter to Santa

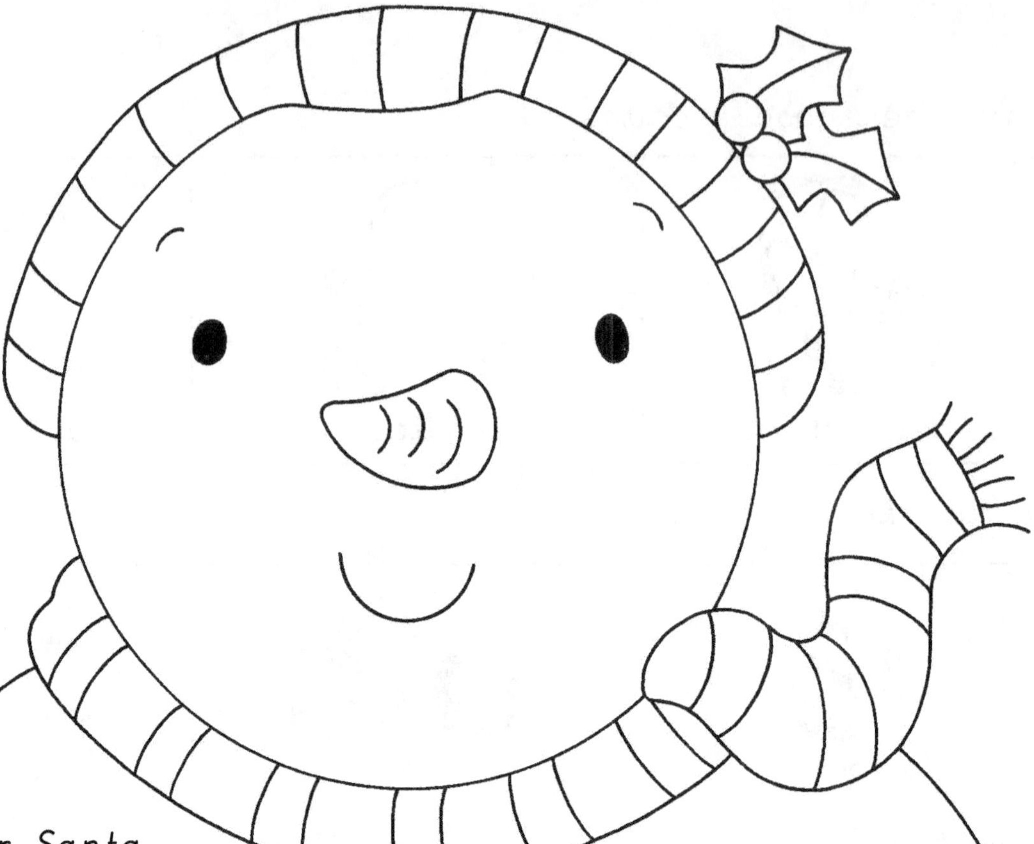

Dear Santa,

I have been good because I

I would like

I have left you a ______________________ and

______________________ for the reindeer.

Love from,

Book review

Title

Author

What was the story about?

Who was your favourite character and why?

Which part of the story did you like best?

Who would like this story?

How many stars would you give this book?

Boost Creative Writing, Years 1–2
© Judith Thornby and Brilliant Publications Limited

This page may be photocopied for use by the purchasing institution only.

A review of Year 2

Interesting starting sentence

Ideas:
It has been good fun in Year 2.
I have really enjoyed Year 2.

What have you done so far? Why did you like doing it?

Ideas:
trip to...
class assembly
performance

What are your favourite lessons? Why?

Is there anything you are not so keen on? Why?

What are you getting better at?

What will you miss when you go up into Year 3?

What are you looking forward to in Year 3?

Ideas:
new lessons   teachers

Rain

Write a rhyming poem about the rain. Use the words in bold as the first line in each rhyming pair. Write the next line. Don't forget it must end with a rhyming word.

For example:
Split spl<u>at</u>
I will not sit on the m<u>at</u>.

Use this sheet to think of lots of rhyming words.

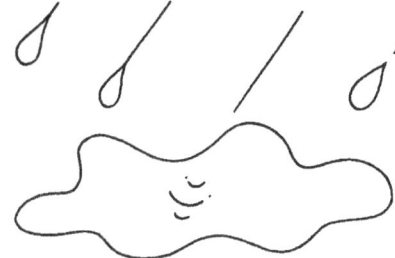

Split spl<u>at</u>

My rhyming words

Drip dr<u>op</u>

My rhyming words

Splish spl<u>ash</u>

My rhyming words

Splash spl<u>ish</u>

My rhyming words

Pitter p<u>atter</u>

My rhyming words

You can use these words!

| h<u>at</u> | c<u>at</u> | sh<u>op</u> | h<u>op</u> | d<u>ash</u> |
| m<u>ash</u> | f<u>ish</u> | w<u>ish</u> | ch<u>atter</u> | m<u>atter</u> |

Boost Creative Writing, Years 1–2
© Judith Thornby and Brilliant Publications Limited

Rain

by ....

....

....

....

....

....

....

....

....

....

....

My home

What do you like to do in your home?

I like to .... in the	/k/ cook camp cry
I like to .... in the	/l/ lie down laugh
I like to .... in the	/h/ hop help

Choose a room:
living room   hall   bedroom   dining room
toilet   kitchen   cloakroom   study

I like to .... in the	☐
I like to .... in the	☐
I like to .... in the	☐
I like to .... in the	☐
	☐

Boost Creative Writing, Years 1–2
© Judith Thornby and Brilliant Publications Limited

Grandad

Write a funny rhyming poem. Create a pretend conversation between a child and a grandad who is deaf.

For example:
Tom: Do you want me to get your cap?
Grandad: No, the cat is on my lap.

Tom: Shall I go and get us a cake?
Grandad: No, do not get a snake!

Tom: Can I buy you a drink?
Grandad: No, I do not need a new sink.

Tom: Are you feeling well?
Grandad: Yes, I think I can spell.

Start by working out words with the same rhyming patterns. Then think of your sentences. Here are a few to start you off:

ap	nap map clap trap cap lap
ake	cake bake flake Jake lake rake
ink	drink pink rink sink think wink
ell	bell sell shell smell well yell

Grandad

by ....

.... : ....

Grandad: ....

.... : ....

Grandad: ....

.... : ....

Grandad: ....

.... : ....

Grandad: ....

.... : ....

Grandad: ....

Fireworks

Play around with 'noisy' words and make up a fireworks poem.

For example:
Bang Zoom Boom
Beautiful fireworks
Glittering in the night sky.

Fizzle Sizzle Whizz
Silvery sparklers
Swirling brightly in my hand.

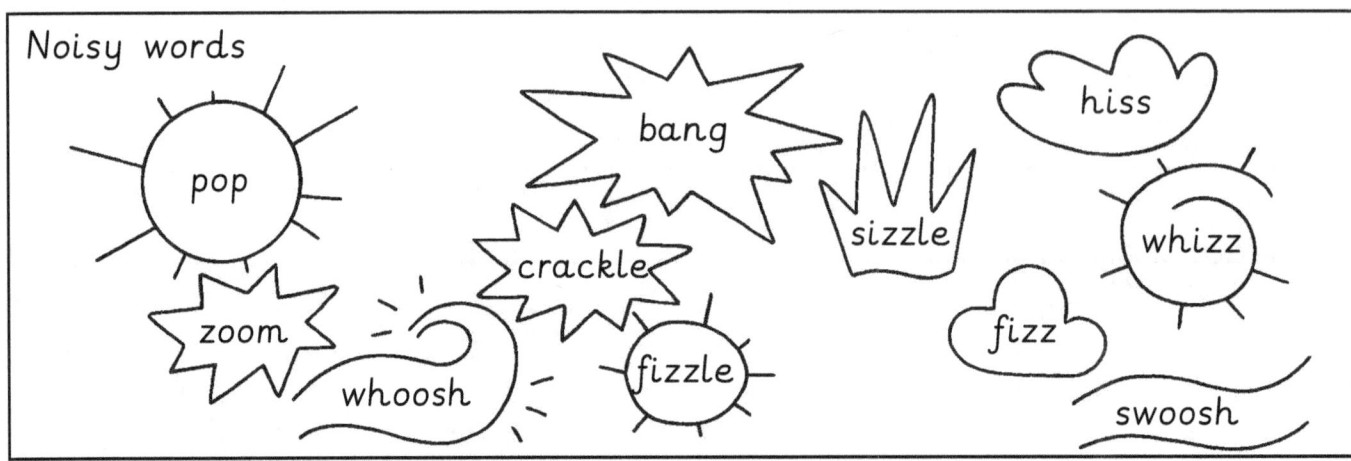

Try to work out your ideas before you write.
Here are some useful words:

colourful amazing	rocket	shooting up blasting off
silvery shining bright	sparks sparklers	glittering sparkling glowing
frightening loud	fire crackers	exploding
beautiful amazing	Roman candle	swirling
wonderful marvellous	Catherine wheel	whizzing around twisting
red hot huge	bonfire	crackling
dark	night sky	appearing disappearing
happy excited	children	admiring loving the sight

Fireworks

by ....

_____

....

....

_____

....

....

_____

....

....

_____

....

....

Noisy words: pop, bang, hiss, crackle, sizzle, whizz, zoom, whoosh, fizzle, fizz

Mini-beasts

Where is it?

on a leaf next to a...	under a stone under a...	in the grass beside the...	by the plant pot near the...

What is it?

ant bee beetle butterfly caterpillar centipede daddy long legs	dragon fly earthworm earwig frog grasshopper green fly ladybird	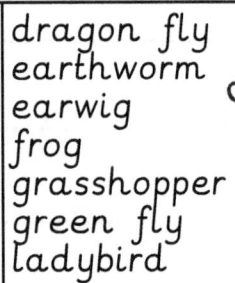 	mosquito moth slug snail spider wasp worm	

What is it doing?

buzzing following fluttering flying	getting gliding guarding looking for	resting returning to scurrying scuttling	searching for sleeping slithering wriggling

Choose a WOW word

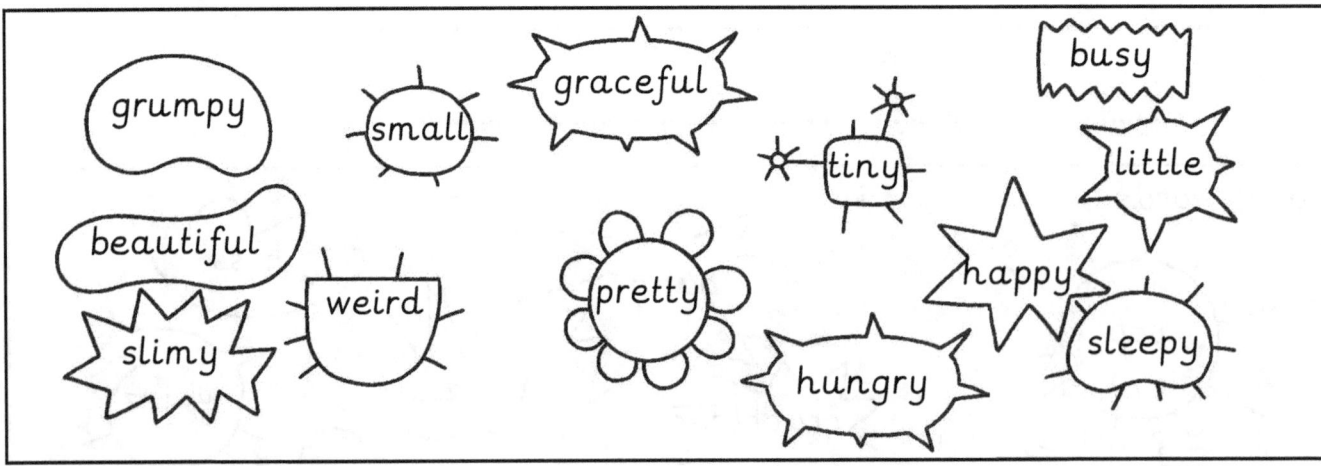

Make up sentences:
Under a flower pot a small woodlouse is sleeping.

Mini-beasts

by _____

Spring

What can you see?

				growing flowering peeping budding
tulip	daffodil	grass	blossom	

What can you see?

	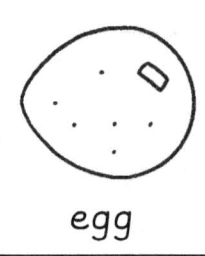		nest building hatching wriggling
bird	egg	worm	

What can you hear?

			croaking cheeping buzzing
chicks	bee	frog	

Choose a WOW word

round, red, long, fresh, yellow, busy, hungry, beautiful, pretty, little, tiny, new, happy, slimy

Make up poem ideas:

New grass growing

Red tulip _____

_____

I can see spring is here.

Spring

by _____

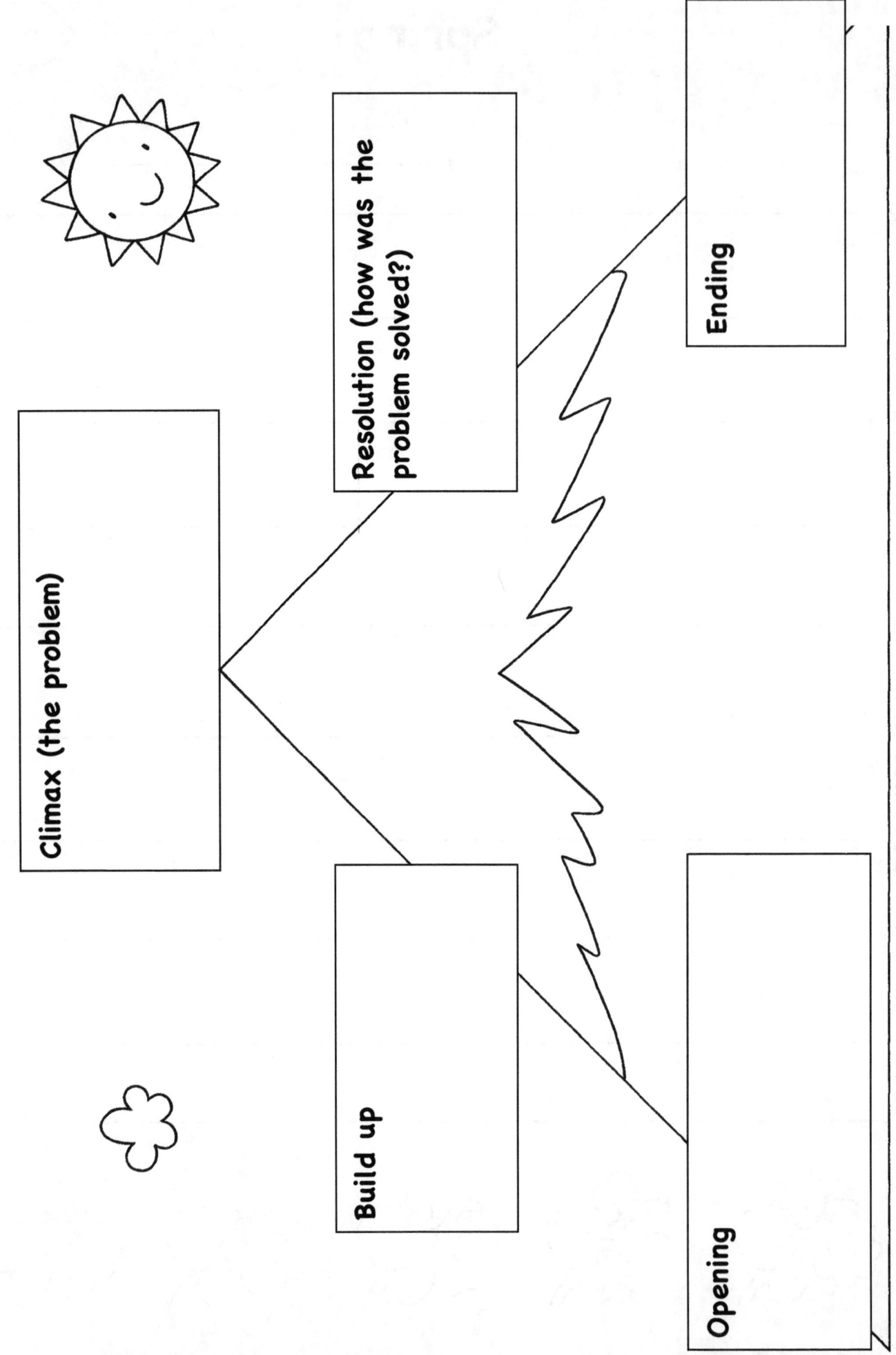

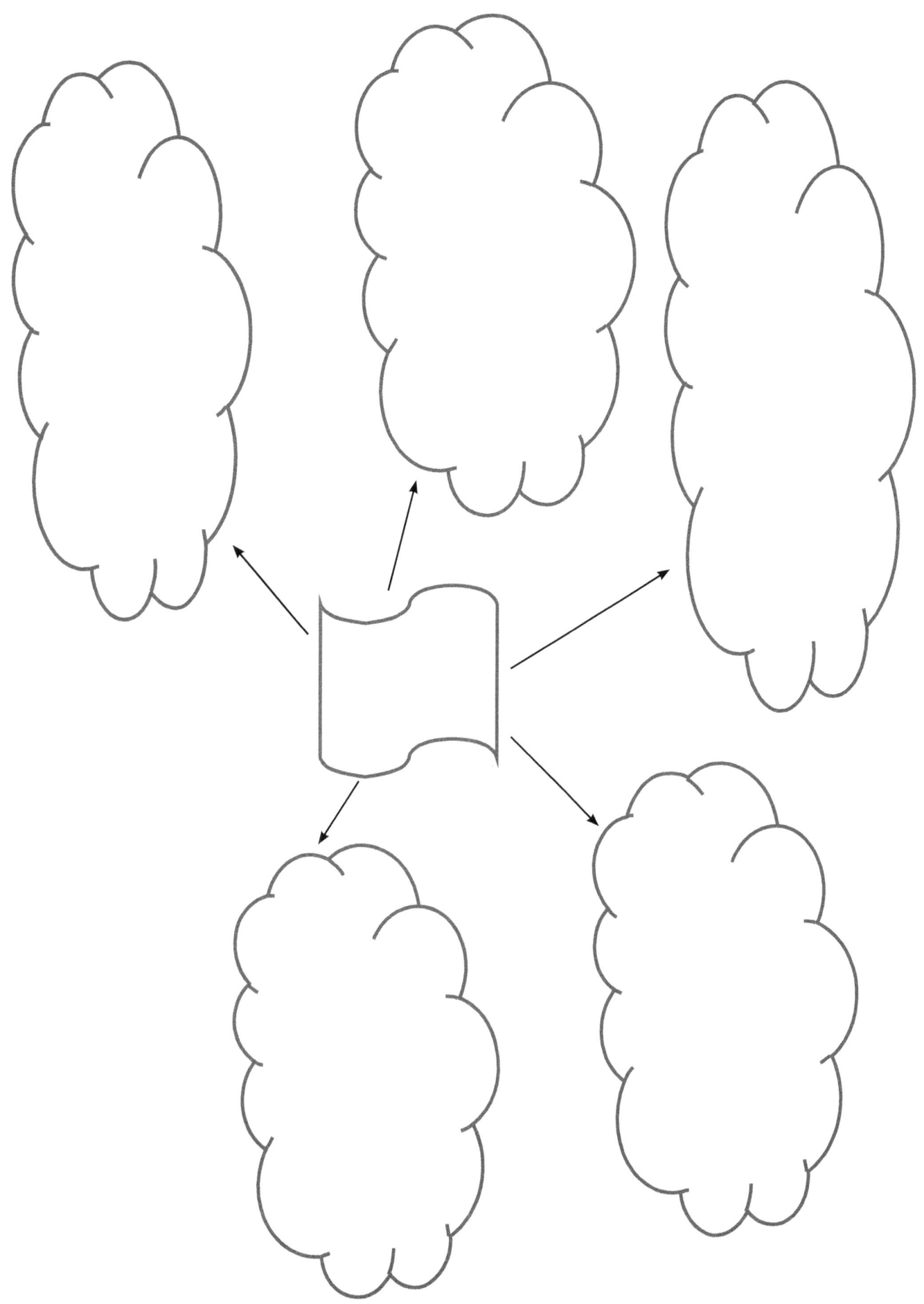

Ages: 7–9yrs

Boost Creative Writing
Planning Sheets to Support Writers (Especially SEN Pupils) in Years 3–4

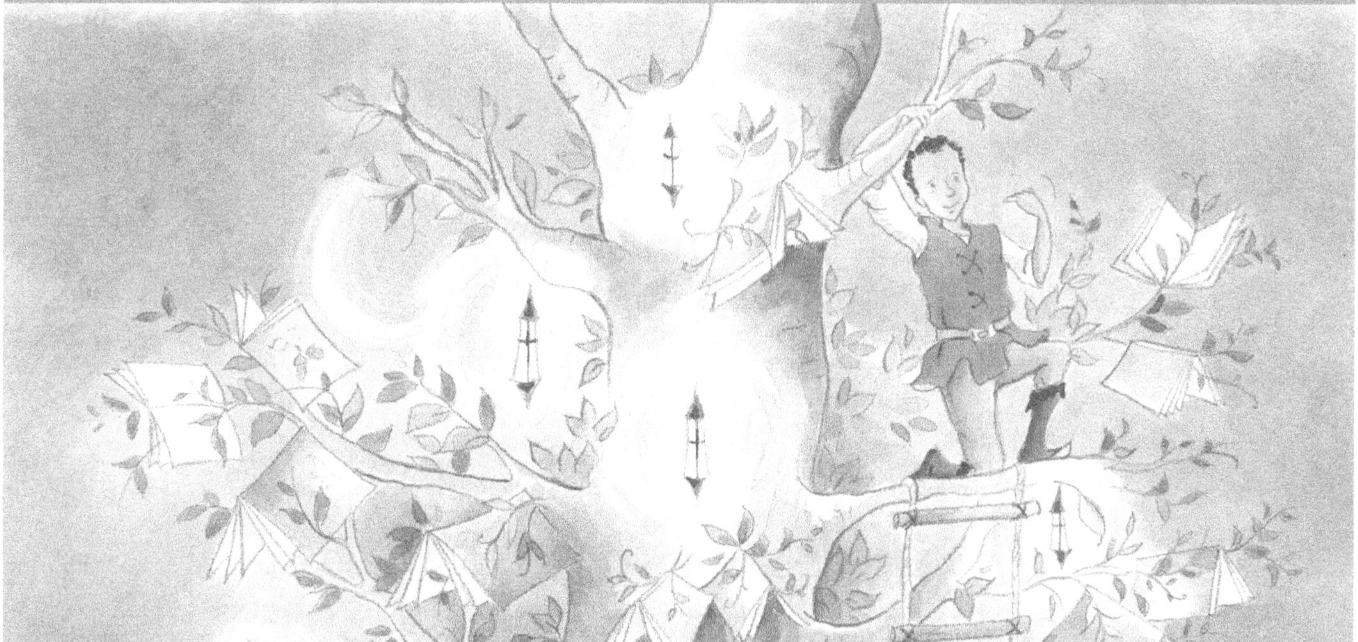

Judith Thornby

Boost Creative Writing

Planning Sheets to Support Writers (Especially SEN Pupils) in Years 3–4

Judith Thornby

We hope you and your pupils enjoy using the ideas in this book. Brilliant Publications publishes many other books to help primary school teachers. To find out more details on all of our titles, including those listed below, please go to our website: www.brilliantpublications.co.uk.

Boost Creative Writing – Years 1–2	978-1-78317-058-6
Boost Creative Writing – Years 5–6	978-1-78317-060-9
Brilliant Activities for Reading Comprehension, Year 1	978-1-78317-070-8
Brilliant Activities for Reading Comprehension, Year 2	978-1-78317-071-5
Brilliant Activities for Reading Comprehension, Year 3	978-1-78317-072-2
Brilliant Activities for Reading Comprehension, Year 4	978-1-78317-073-9
Brilliant Activities for Reading Comprehension, Year 5	978-1-78317-074-6
Brilliant Activities for Reading Comprehension, Year 6	978-1-78317-075-3
Brilliant Activities for Creative Writing, Year 1	978-0-85747-463-6
Brilliant Activities for Creative Writing, Year 2	978-0-85747-464-3
Brilliant Activities for Creative Writing, Year 3	978-0-85747-465-0
Brilliant Activities for Creative Writing, Year 4	978-0-85747-466-7
Brilliant Activities for Creative Writing, Year 5	978-0-85747-467-4
Brilliant Activities for Creative Writing, Year 6	978-0-85747-468-1
Developing Reading Comprehension Skills Years 5-6: Classic Children's Literature	978-0-85747-837-5
Developing Reading Comprehension Skills Years 5-6: Classic Poetry	978-0-85747-846-7
How to Achieve Outstanding Writers in the EYFS and KS1	978-0-85747-838-2
Cracking Creative Writing	978-0-85747-831-3
Boost Spelling Skills	978-0-85747-803-0

Published by Brilliant Publications Limited
Unit 10
Sparrow Hall Farm
Edlesborough
Dunstable
Bedfordshire
LU6 2ES, UK

www.brilliantpublications.co.uk

The name Brilliant Publications and the logo are registered trademarks.

Written by Judith Thornby
Illustrated by Chantal Kees
Cover illustration by Frank Endersby
Designed by Brilliant Publications Limited

© Text Judith Thornby 2014
© Design Brilliant Publications Limited 2014

Printed book ISBN: 978-1-78317-059-3
E-book ISBN: 978-1-78317-062-3

First printed and published in the UK in 2014

The right of Judith Thornby to be identified as the author of this work has been asserted by herself in accordance with the Copyright, Designs and Patents Act 1988.

Pages 6–72 may be copied by individual teachers acting on behalf of the purchasing institution for classroom use only, without permission from the publisher and without declaration to the Copyright Licensing Agency or Publishers' Licensing Services. The materials may not be reproduced in any other form or for any other purpose without the prior permission of the publisher.

Contents

Introduction 4
Links to the National Curriculum 5
Suggested writing targets 6

Adventure story
The box 7–8
The little visitor 9–10
The secret shed 11–12
The time machine 13–14
The unusual plant 15–16
Super shape shifter Sam 17–18
Hidden treasure 19–22
An alien came to dinner 23–24
Adventure in the rainforest 25–26
The genie in a bottle 27–28
The magic tree 29–30

Descriptive account
Wonderland 31–32
The Very Important Person (VIP) 33–34
A day on fantasy island 35–36
The shop of magical things 37–38
Camping out! 39–40
A visit to the dentist 41–42

Traditional tale
The enchanted water 43–45

Fable/myth
My mythical creature 46–47
My myth 48
One good turn deserves another 49

Poetry
Granny – a rhyming poem 50–51
A haiku riddle 52
Winter 53–54

Letter
A seasonal letter 55
A chatty letter 56
A letter to an author 57

Review
A book review 58

Report/recount
My favourite pet animal 59–60
The Ancient Greeks 61
Iron Age Celts 62
My newspaper report 63–64

Instructional writing
How to make pancakes 65
Make a super sandwich 66

Roald Dahl
The clever trick 67–68
Mr Twit's trick 69–70

Templates
Story mountain template 71
Mind map template 72

Introduction

These series of planning sheets aim to provide a structured resource which gives plenty of scope for exploring and collecting ideas in the different writing genres: adventure, fantasy, recount, letter, poetry etc. They generate discussion within a defined framework and then aid pupils to write more descriptive stories and compose longer pieces of writing.

Reluctant writers or those writers who struggle with the organization of their ideas can express themselves with more self-assurance by using these planning sheets. Confident writers can also benefit by delving into them to gain further ideas.

Some sheets can be written on directly but many are designed as a prop to refer to when writing. Vocabulary sheets are incorporated with some stories to help the flow of ideas.

Story mountain and mind map templates are included to assist narrative and descriptive writing and to cater for different learning styles. Visual learners have lots of imaginative ideas but might struggle with the sequence of events or the bare skeleton of the story so can benefit from using the story mountain approach. Logical systematic learners can sequence ideas but might struggle to develop them creatively and can benefit from using the mind map templates to expand descriptive writing.

I have specialized in the field of learning support since 1997 when I gained a diploma in specific learning difficulties. I am especially interested in promoting creative writing skills with children who are reluctant writers or who struggle with the organization of their ideas. These series of planning sheets generate discussion and aid in structuring composition in the different writing genres. They also can be used to give further ideas to confident writers as well. I have found that they have been successful in giving pupils greater self-assurance to express themselves in written form and have helped to make writing an enjoyable experience!

On page 5 you will see how the activities in the book link to the 2014 National Curriculum for England. On page 6 there are suggested writing targets. The way I use these is to cut out the relevant one(s) and tape them to the top of the sheets prior to copying, so that pupils have the targets in front of them as they work.

Links to the National Curriculum

The sheets in **Boost Creative Writing** will help Year 3 and 4 pupils to develop their composition skills, as set out in the National Curriculum for England (2014).

Composition

The sheets in **Boost Creative Writing** help pupils to plan their writing, by providing a structured format for discussing and recording their ideas. Some sample pieces of writing are given, but pupils would benefit from discussing and analysing the structure, vocabulary and grammar used in other similar texts.

All pupils, but especially SEN pupils, will find it very beneficial to have the opportunity to talk about what they are going to write prior to doing so, as often pupils' writing ability lags behind their speaking ability. Composing and rehearsing sentences orally, prior to writing, helps them to build a varied and rich vocabulary and encourages an increased range of sentence structures.

The sheets in this book can be used to help children to become aware of, and start to use, features of writing. In narratives, the structured format of the sheets encourages them to think and talk about the setting, characters and plot. Similarly, for non-narrative pieces, the way the sheets are formatted encourages pupils to think about how they will structure their writing.

When pupils have finished their writing, they should be encouraged to re-read their work and to think about how it can be improved. Discussing their work with you and with other pupils will help them to assess the effectiveness of their own writing.

Reading their writing aloud helps children to see that their writing is valued. Encourage pupils to use appropriate intonation and to control the tone and volume so that the meaning is clear.

Vocabulary, grammar and punctuation

Many of the sheets contain suggested vocabulary to encourage children to extend their range of vocabulary and prompt them to use new words in their writing. The activities can also be used to reinforce children's understanding of grammar and punctuation, but this is not the primary purpose of the sheets.

Suggested writing targets

To have an opening, middle and ending in my writing
To understand how to use paragraphs in my writing
To understanding the story mountain structure of narrative writing: opening, build up, climax, resolution, ending
To discuss and plan my story before writing using a story mountain or mind map
To use interesting verbs when writing the build-up part of the story
To use powerful adjectives in a description
To describe a character in detail
To describe a setting in detail
To use a range of adjectives, powerful verbs and adverbs to make the description sparkle
To understand the main ways authors use to start a story: setting, character, speech, statement
To write 3 different types of story starters, eg descriptions of character or setting or a question
To write an interesting opening paragraph with a hook to keep the reader interested
To check that I am writing in the same tense
To read over my writing, checking that I have put in capital letters and full stops
To use time connectives to start my sentences in different ways: Then... Suddenly... Next minute... Meanwhile... Eventually...
To use speech marks correctly and start a new line when someone is speaking
To use a repeating line in a poem
To plan and write an information booklet
To recount real events in the order they happened
To set out an address correctly and set out a letter correctly (both formal and informal)
To write a descriptive poem using personification or simile to paint an image in words
To use sensory description in my writing – What can you see? hear? smell? taste? How are you feeling?
To use connectives to elongate my sentences
To make up my own recipe using imperative verbs (bossy verbs)
To establish a different viewpoint in writing
To present different sides of a viewpoint

This page may be photocopied for use by the purchasing institution only.

The box

Write a story about a person who heard a loud knock on the door. When he or she opened the door, there was an unusual-looking box on the doorstep.

Who heard the knock? Where? What was the person doing?

What did the box look like?
Ideas: size?   wrapped in?   ribbon?   label?

What was in the box?
Ideas:

What happened that was a bit extraordinary? Then? After that?
Ideas: a magic carpet took you to a different place
a genie came out of the lamp
a toy came alive

What happened at the end?

Boost Creative Writing, Years 3–4
© Judith Thornby and Brilliant Publications Limited

The box

Adventure story

Put a short draft of your main ideas into each box using the story mountain format.

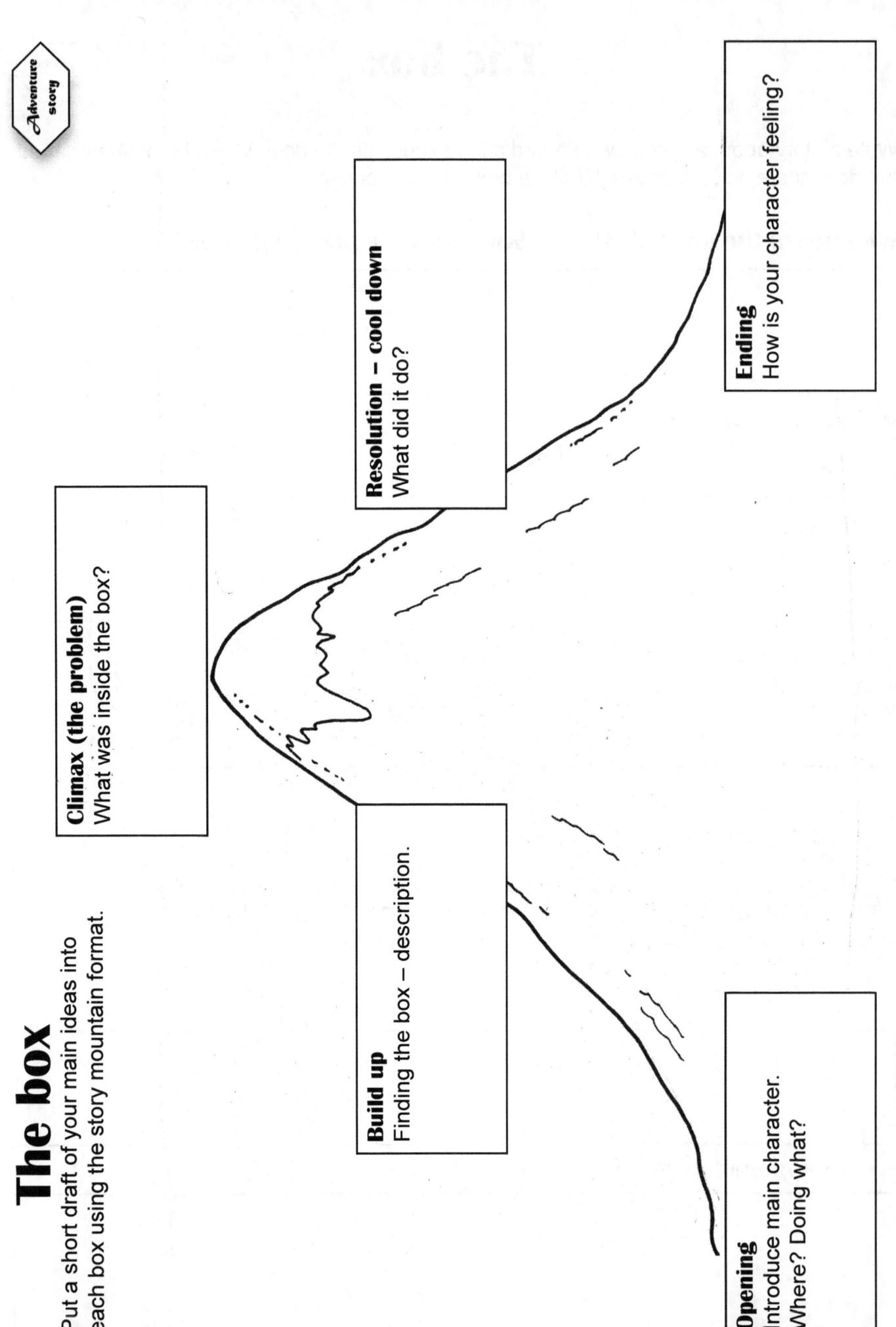

Climax (the problem)
What was inside the box?

Resolution – cool down
What did it do?

Ending
How is your character feeling?

Build up
Finding the box – description.

Opening
Introduce main character.
Where? Doing what?

The little visitor

Write a story about a someone who was just getting ready for school when he or she met an odd-looking little person.

Who was getting ready for school?

It was early one sunny morning and .... was eating breakfast in the kitchen when he/she noticed a rather odd-looking person in the back garden.

Describe the little person in detail.
Idea: He had wrinkled skin and very large ears.

What happened next?
Ideas:　　the alien took the person to school in his spaceship
　　　　　the gnome went to school in a satchel

What happened after that? What lessons did the little visitor go to? Did something surprising happen?

What happened at the end?

Boost Creative Writing, Years 3–4
© Judith Thornby and Brilliant Publications Limited

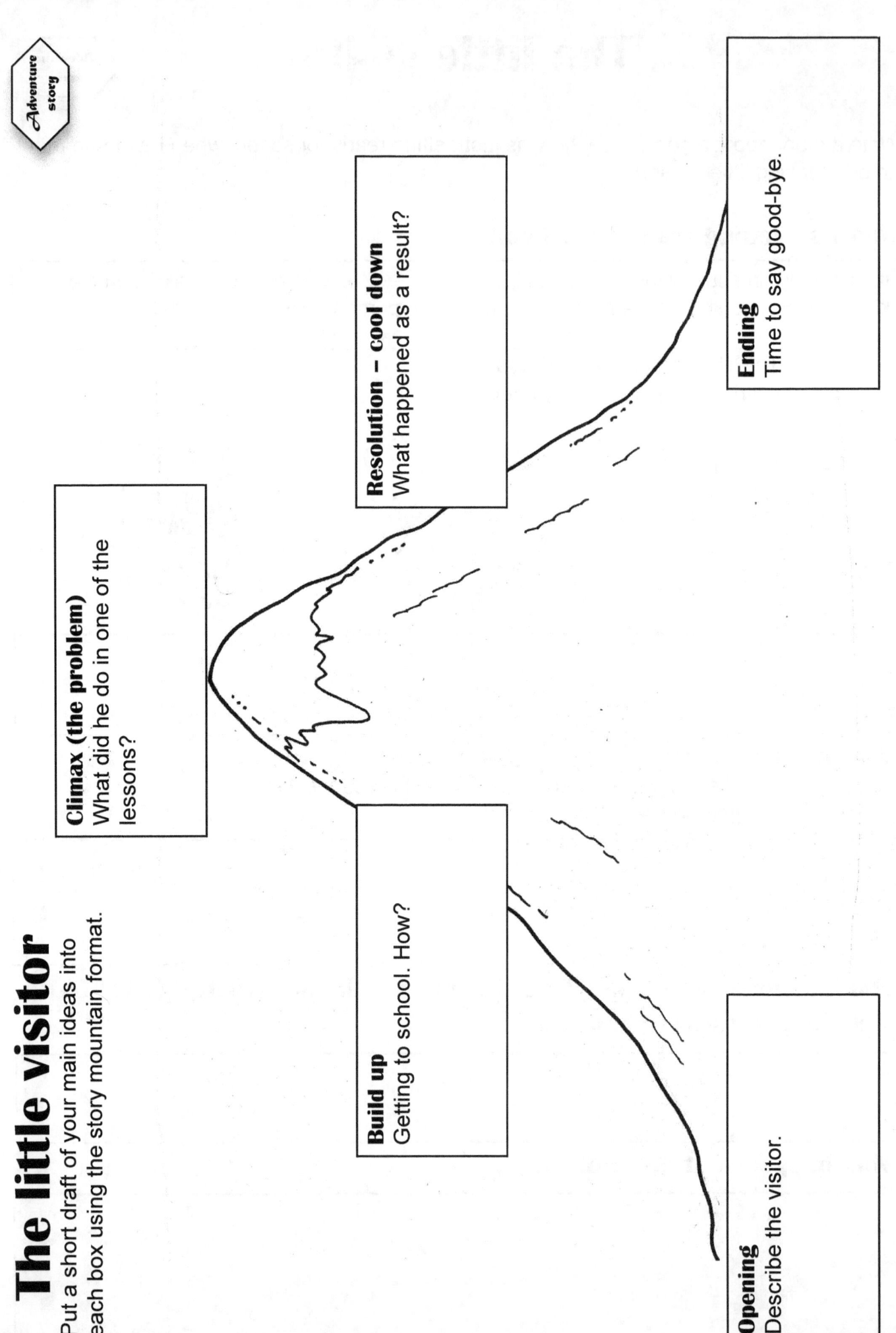

Adventure story

The little visitor

Put a short draft of your main ideas into each box using the story mountain format.

Opening
Describe the visitor.

Build up
Getting to school. How?

Climax (the problem)
What did he do in one of the lessons?

Resolution – cool down
What happened as a result?

Ending
Time to say good-bye.

The secret shed

Write a story about a someone who finds something rather special in a garden outbuilding.

The outbuilding was half hidden by climbing roses at the bottom of my Grandad's large garden. I had never noticed it before today. I pushed on the door, but it was tightly locked. I just had to find the key so I could find out what was inside.

Where did I look for the key?
What did the key look like?
Idea: Think of three places.

What was in the shed?
Ideas:

What happened next? Then? After that?
Ideas: your painting came alive
           the mirror was magic and made you different
           the dragon blew a fireball and caused a bonfire
           the dragon gave you a ride

What happened at the end?

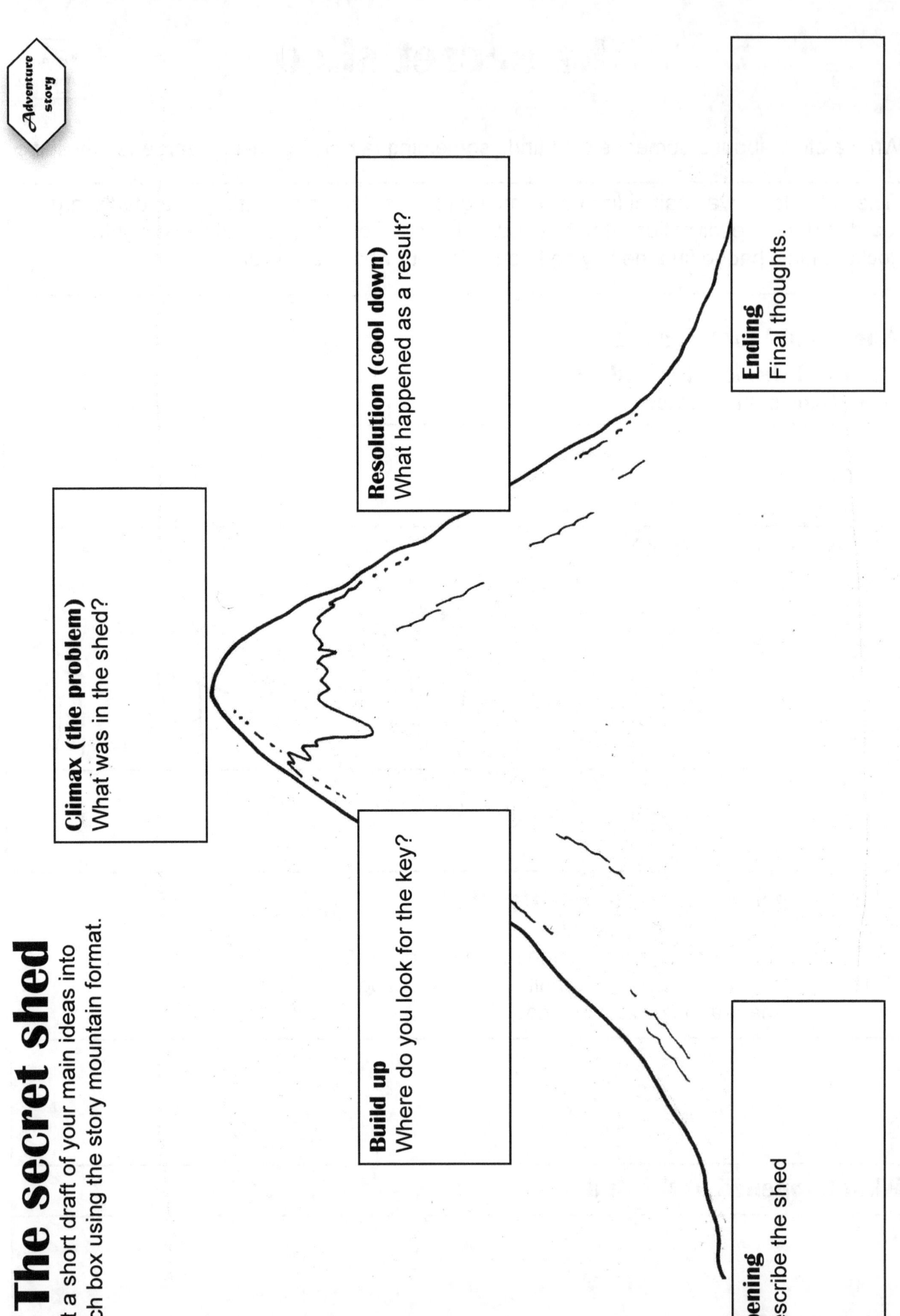

The time machine

Write a story about two children who discovered a time machine and were transported to a different time.

Who were they?

What were they doing? Where did they find the time machine?
Ideas: in the high street   in the park   in the garden   in an antique shop

What did it look like? How did they get into it? How did it start?

Where did they go? What happened next? After that?
Ideas: into the past
         into the future
         to a strange planet

How does the story end? Do they have a reminder of their trip?

Boost Creative Writing, Years 3–4
© Judith Thornby and Brilliant Publications Limited

Adventure story

The time machine

Put a short draft of your main ideas into each box using the story mountain format.

Climax (the problem)
Where does the time machine take them?

Resolution (cool down)
What happened as a result?

Build up
Going inside the machine. How? What?

Ending
A reminder of their trip.

Opening
Where do they find the time machine?

The unusual plant

Write a story about a strange plant and how it caused something unusual to happen in a back garden of a family home.

Opening

The spiny leaves of the large ugly cactus swayed slightly in the light breeze. It shivered in anticipation. The garden it grew in was not deserted anymore, because now the Robinson family had moved in…

What happened first?
Ideas: someone dropped a sock on the plant and didn't notice
the family was having a picnic and a drink was accidentally spilt on the plant

What happened overnight?
Ideas: tiny socks start growing on the plant
little cups grow on the plant

What happened next?
Ideas: the socks smell – and then?
the cups fill up with a favourite drink – and then?

What happens at the end?

Boost Creative Writing, Years 3–4

Adventure story

The unusual plant

Put a short draft of your main ideas into each box using the story mountain format.

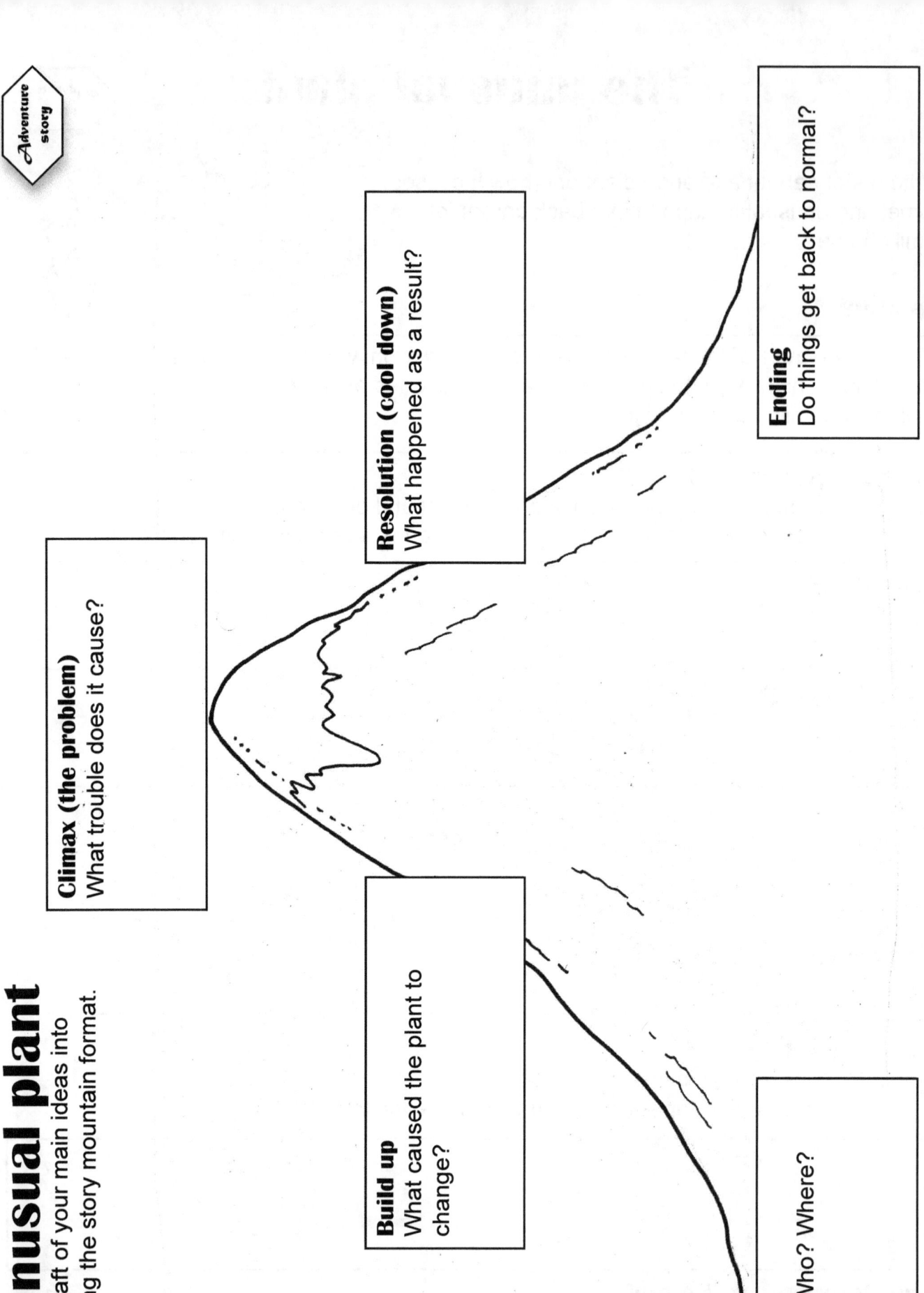

Climax (the problem)
What trouble does it cause?

Resolution (cool down)
What happened as a result?

Build up
What caused the plant to change?

Ending
Do things get back to normal?

Opening
Characters: Who? Where?

This page may be photocopied for use by the purchasing institution only.

Boost Creative Writing, Years 3–4
© Judith Thornby and Brilliant Publications Limited

Super shape shifter Sam

When Sam ate the cupcake he bought at 'The Super Cupcake Shop' this morning, he didn't know that it would give him super shape shifting powers every time he got nervous.

Describe the cupcake
How did it smell? look? taste?

How did Sam feel as soon as he had eaten it?
Ideas: toes tingled   face felt red

A little while later
What made Sam feel nervous at school? Why?
Ideas: Mrs Hotpepper, the maths teacher   Jake Higsbottom, the school bully

What did Sam change shape to?
Ideas: a mouse   a giant

What happened next? After that?

How did the story end?
Did the shape shifter power last?

Adventure story

Super shape shifter Sam

Put a short draft of your main ideas into each box using the story mountain format.

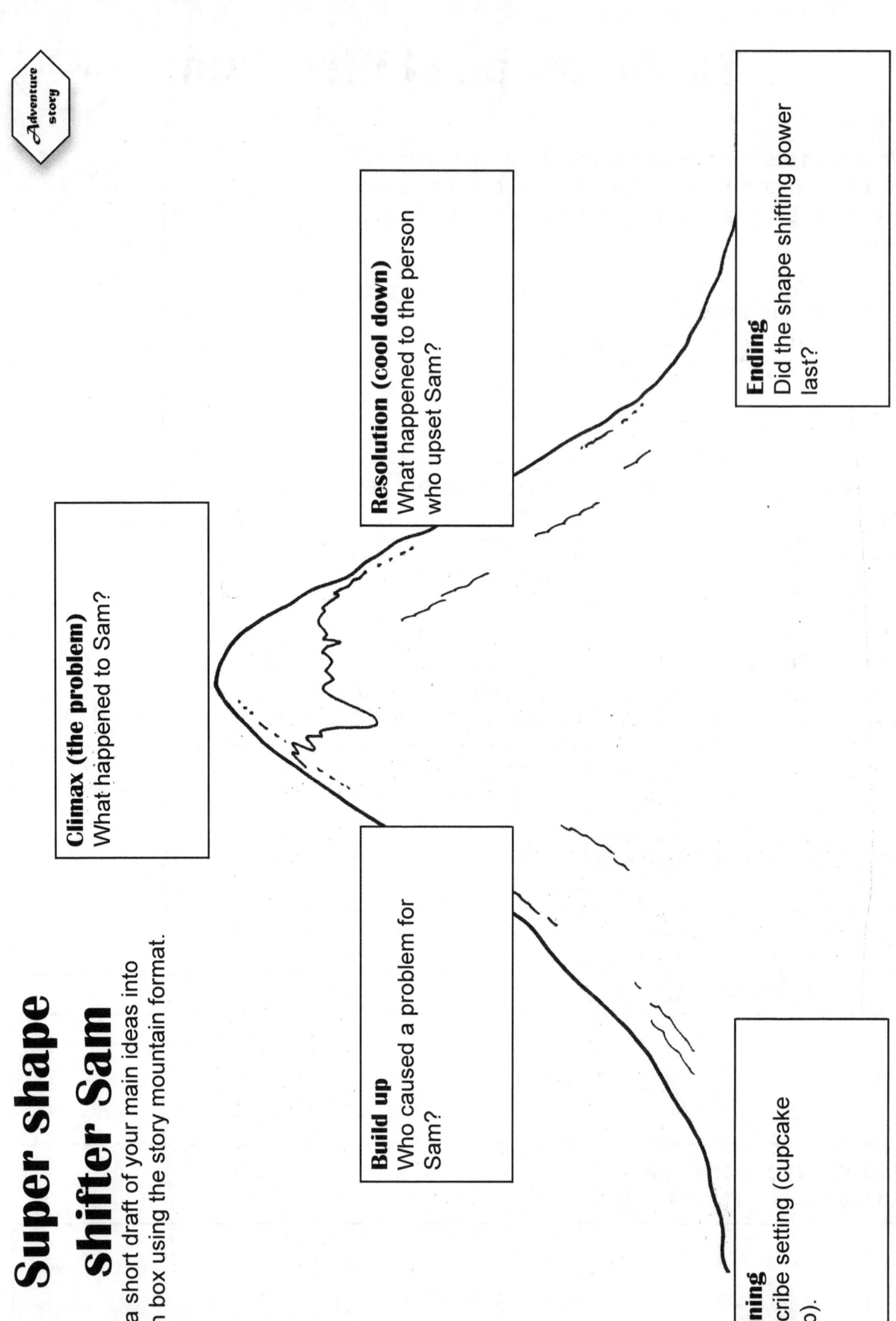

Climax (the problem)
What happened to Sam?

Resolution (cool down)
What happened to the person who upset Sam?

Ending
Did the shape shifting power last?

Build up
Who caused a problem for Sam?

Opening
Describe setting (cupcake shop).

This page may be photocopied for use by the purchasing institution only.

Hidden treasure

Write a story about a pirate looking for treasure on an island.

Who?
Describe the pirate in detail.

Setting

Idea:
The pirate ship _____ floated silently into the deserted bay Captain _____ really hoped he had found the right island at long last…

Vocabulary:
squidgy sands, misty forest, tall trees, wrecked rope bridge, eerie red lake, cavernous cave, massive footprints, animal (what type?), treasure

What problems did the pirate have to overcome?

Ideas:
sunk in squishy sand – able to grab hold of a rock
got lost in a misty forest – monkey helped to find the way
fell into eerie red lake – giant turtle offered a ride
caught in a huge storm – sheltered in a cave

What was the treasure? Where was it found?

Ideas: gold coins   rare or extinct animal   special plant   tree dwelling natives

Was it what the pirate expected?
What were the pirate's thoughts about the treasure?

Adventure story

Hidden treasure

Put a short draft of your main ideas into each box using the story mountain format.

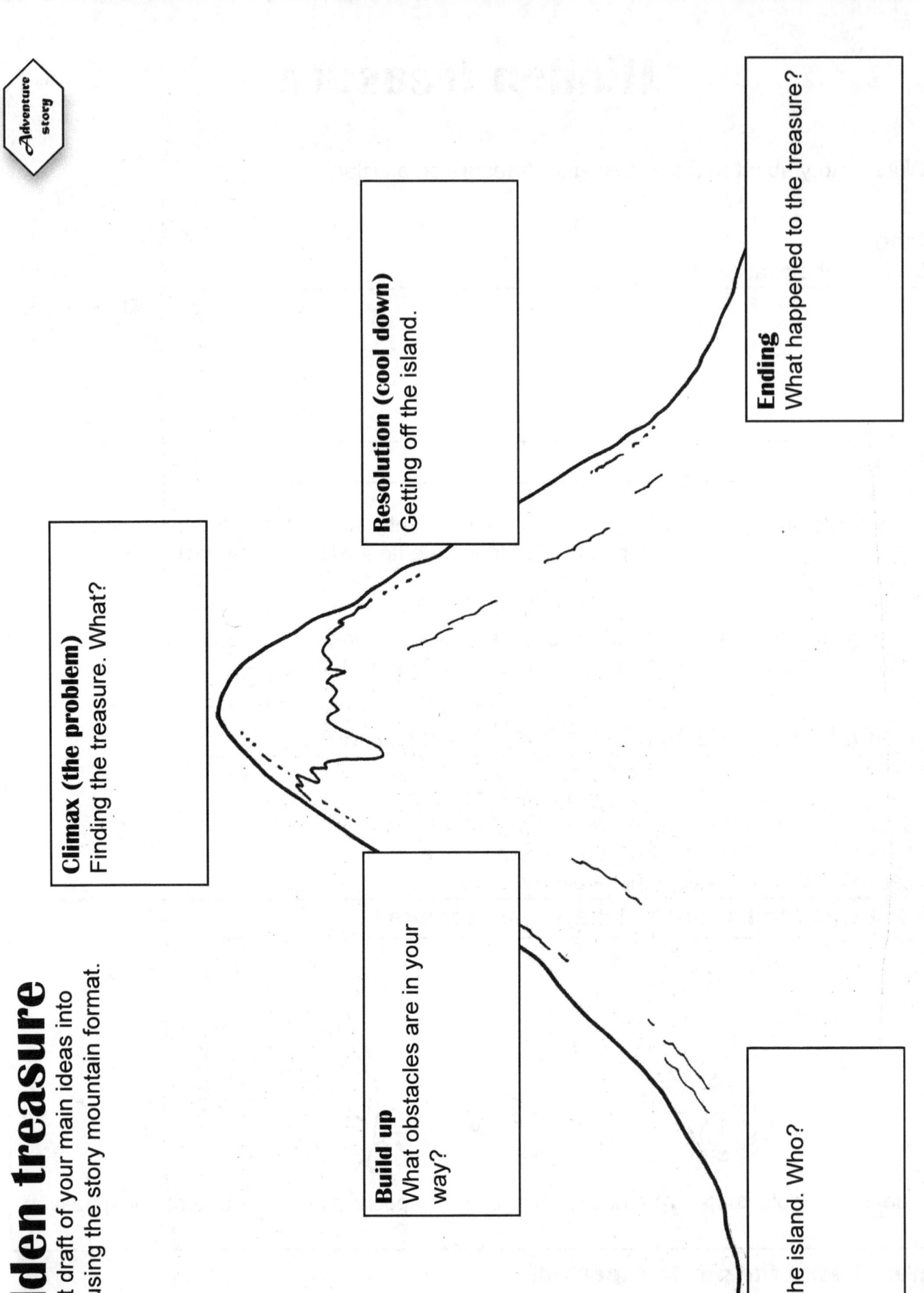

Climax (the problem)
Finding the treasure. What?

Resolution (cool down)
Getting off the island.

Build up
What obstacles are in your way?

Opening
Arrival at the island. Who?

Ending
What happened to the treasure?

This page may be photocopied for use by the purchasing institution only.

Boost Creative Writing, Years 3–4
© Judith Thornby and Brilliant Publications Limited

Hidden treasure

Adventure story

Draw and label a map of the island Use **powerful** adjectives to describe the setting. Don't forget **X** marks the treasure on your map!

Vocabulary:

sinking sand	sharp rocks	misty moor	weird woods	tall trees
broken bridge	eerie lake	high hills	cavernous cave	
massive footprints	treasure chest	animal (what type?)		

Hidden treasure

Draw and label a picture of a pirate. Use **powerful** adjectives in the description. What is the pirate's name? What is the name of the pirate's boat?

Pirate's name: _____
(Captain Seawash, Jake Greybeard, etc)

Name of pirate's boat: _____

Vocabulary:
fearsome looking person, scar on face, eye patch, hook hand, wooden leg (What caused it to happen?), hair (greasy, dirty, etc), beard (spiky, bristly, etc), earring (silver, golden), shirt (torn, striped, etc), bandana (spotted, purple, etc), carried a cutlass/parrot

An alien came to dinner

Adventure story

It was just about dinner time when an alien friend of mine flew his spaceship through my open bedroom window and asked for my help.

Who was the alien?

Name? Where did he come from? What did he look like?

Ideas: Quaver Fattystuff from Planet Puff, Zuke Moonwalker from Planet Lunar

What was the problem? What did he want from you?

Ideas:
His spaceship was faulty – did you have something that he could use to mend his ship?
His planet was being attacked by another alien force – Did you have something that would help him to win the battle (maybe food or drink the alien force was allergic to)?

Dinner time!

Was your family happy to see the alien?
What did you have for dinner?
Could the alien eat human food? What did he eat?

What happened after dinner? How did you help the alien?

What happened a few days later, after the alien had gone back to his planet?

Did you get a message or gift, thanking you for your help? Is everything OK now?

Boost Creative Writing, Years 3–4
© Judith Thornby and Brilliant Publications Limited

Adventure story

An alien came to dinner

Put a short draft of your main ideas into each box using the story mountain format.

Climax (the problem)
What's the alien's problem?

Resolution (cool down)
How could you help?

Build up
Down to dinner.

Ending
Thank you message or gift.

Opening
Description of the alien.

Adventure in the rainforest

My aeroplane crashed in a remote area of the Amazon rainforest. Miraculously, I was unhurt, just a bit bruised.

Setting: What was it like in the rainforest?

What can you see? hear?

Ideas: red howler monkey growling, crocodile snapping its teeth, green tree python rustling over leaves, insects chirruping
Vocabulary: dark thick forest of trees, hot, steamy, wet, huge plants, glossy leaves

Problems

Ideas: hunger, plague of mosquitoes bites you, poison arrow frog chases you, someone shoots at you with a poison-tipped arrow

What helps?

Ideas: banana tree, mangoes, pineapple, passion fruit, leaf from a healing medicine plant, shelter behind a waterfall, hide in huge buttress roots of tree

How did you get out of the forest?

Ideas: use wood, vines and leaves to build a canoe, friendly native guides you out

Final thoughts

Will you ever forget this adventure?

Boost Creative Writing, Years 3–4
© Judith Thornby and Brilliant Publications Limited

Adventure in the rainforest

Put a short draft of your main ideas into each box using the story mountain format.

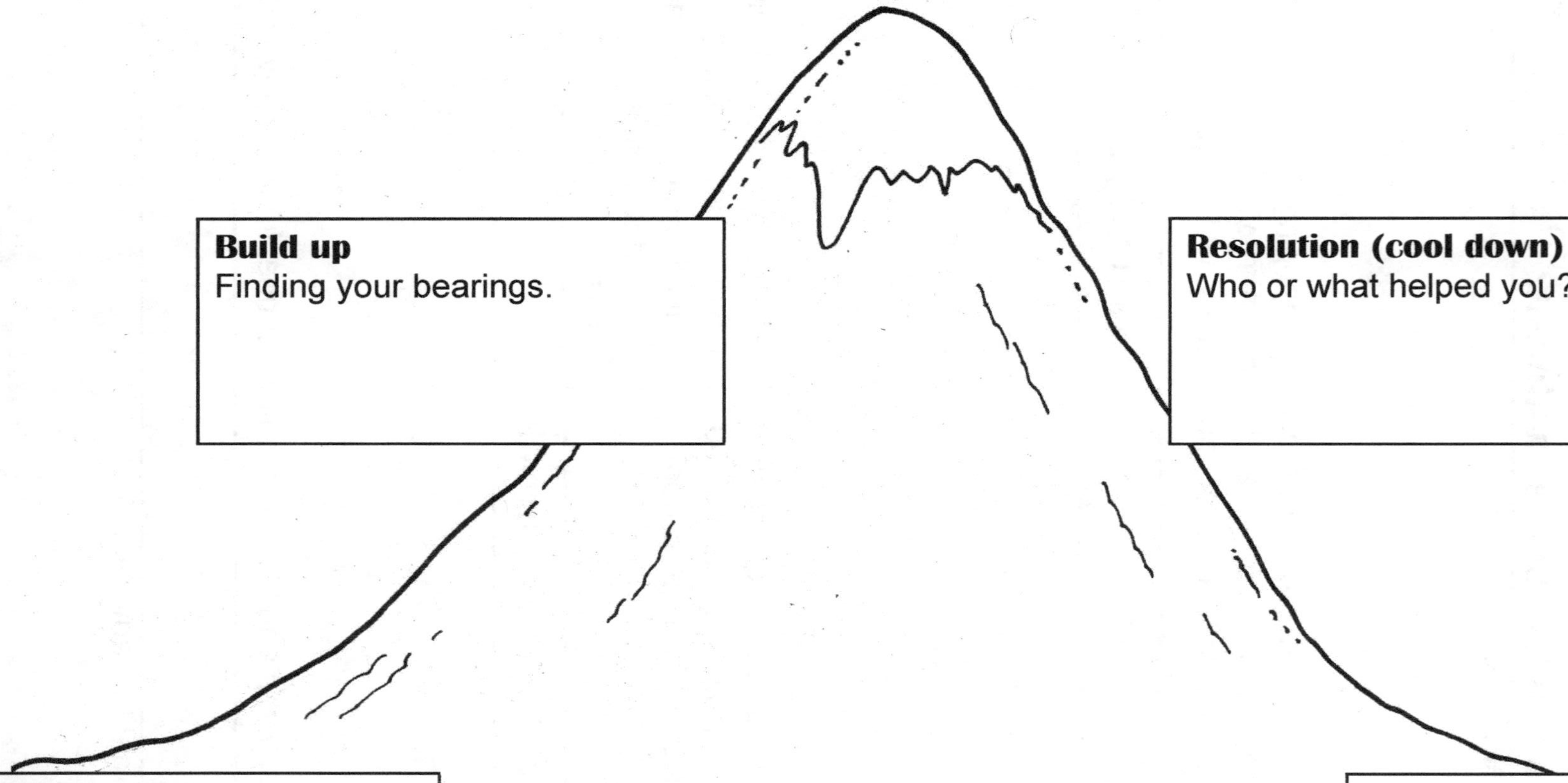

Climax (the problem)
Who or what tried to hurt you?

Resolution (cool down)
Who or what helped you?

Ending
How did you feel?

Build up
Finding your bearings.

Opening
Describe the jungle. What could you see? hear?

The genie in a bottle

Write a story about someone who finds a bottle that has a genie inside it.

Where was the bottle found? What did it look like?
Add detail.

Ideas: at the bottom of a rock pool, amongst the pebbles on the beach, half buried in the sand

Who found it?

What happens when the bottle is rubbed or when the cork is taken out?
Who was in the bottle?

Describe in detail.

What was the wish?

Did it happen straight away?

What happens as a result of the wish?
Was it a good thing or not quite what was expected?

How does the story end?

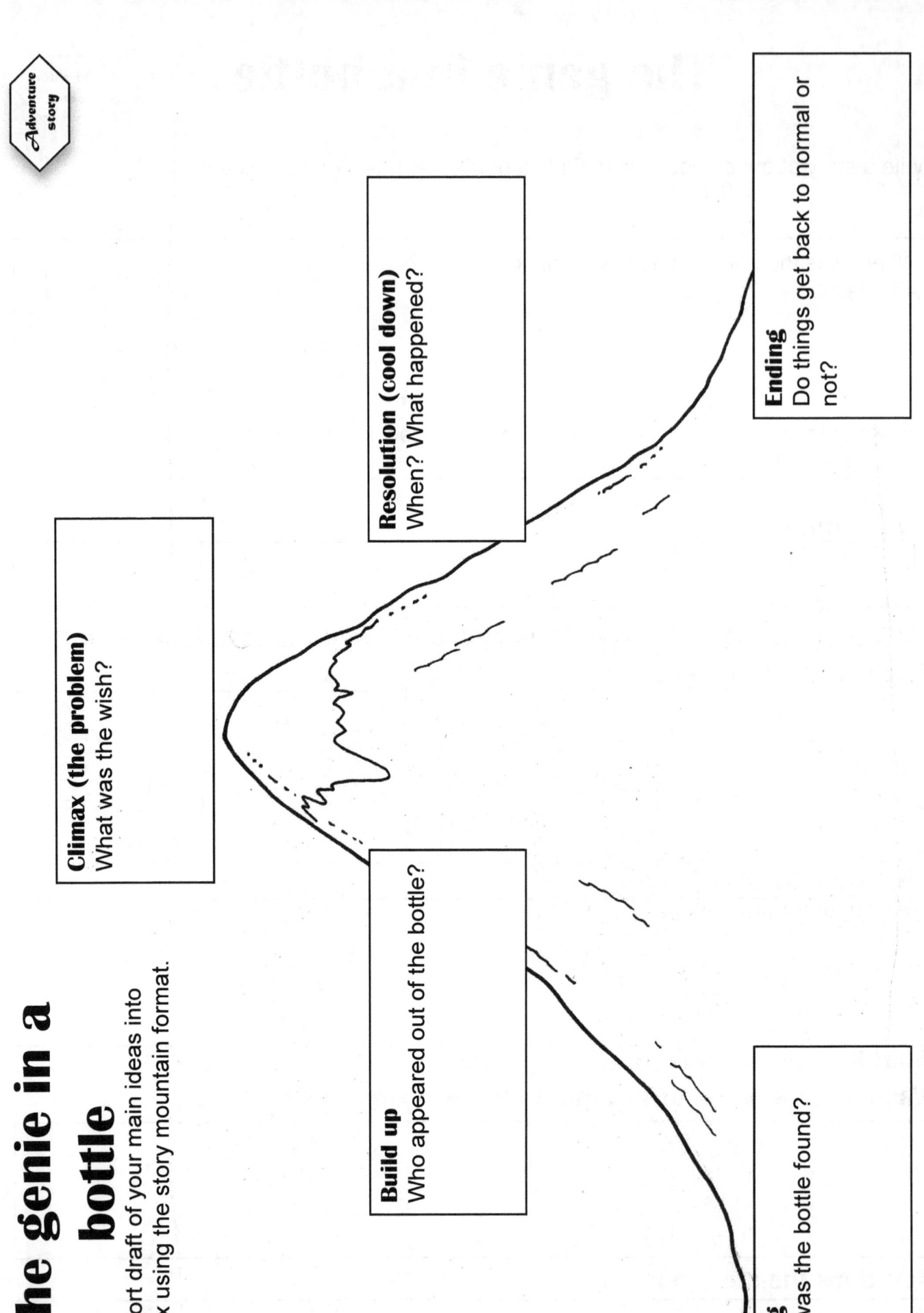

The magic tree

Adventure story

Write a story about a person who finds a magic reading tree with books growing from its branches. What happens when the person meets a character from one of the books?

Describe the setting – Where is it? What time of day?

Ideas: It was quite early in the morning… It was twilight…

What did the tree look like?

Trunk? Bark? Leaves?

Ideas:
The tree had a spotted trunk like a leopard…
It was covered in fairy lights that glowed like…

Who found the tree?

How did he/she meet the character from a book?

Ideas: a ladder appeared… climbed… saw favourite book… opened a page…

Who was the book character?

What happened next?

Is the character worried or excited about anything?

What happened at the end?

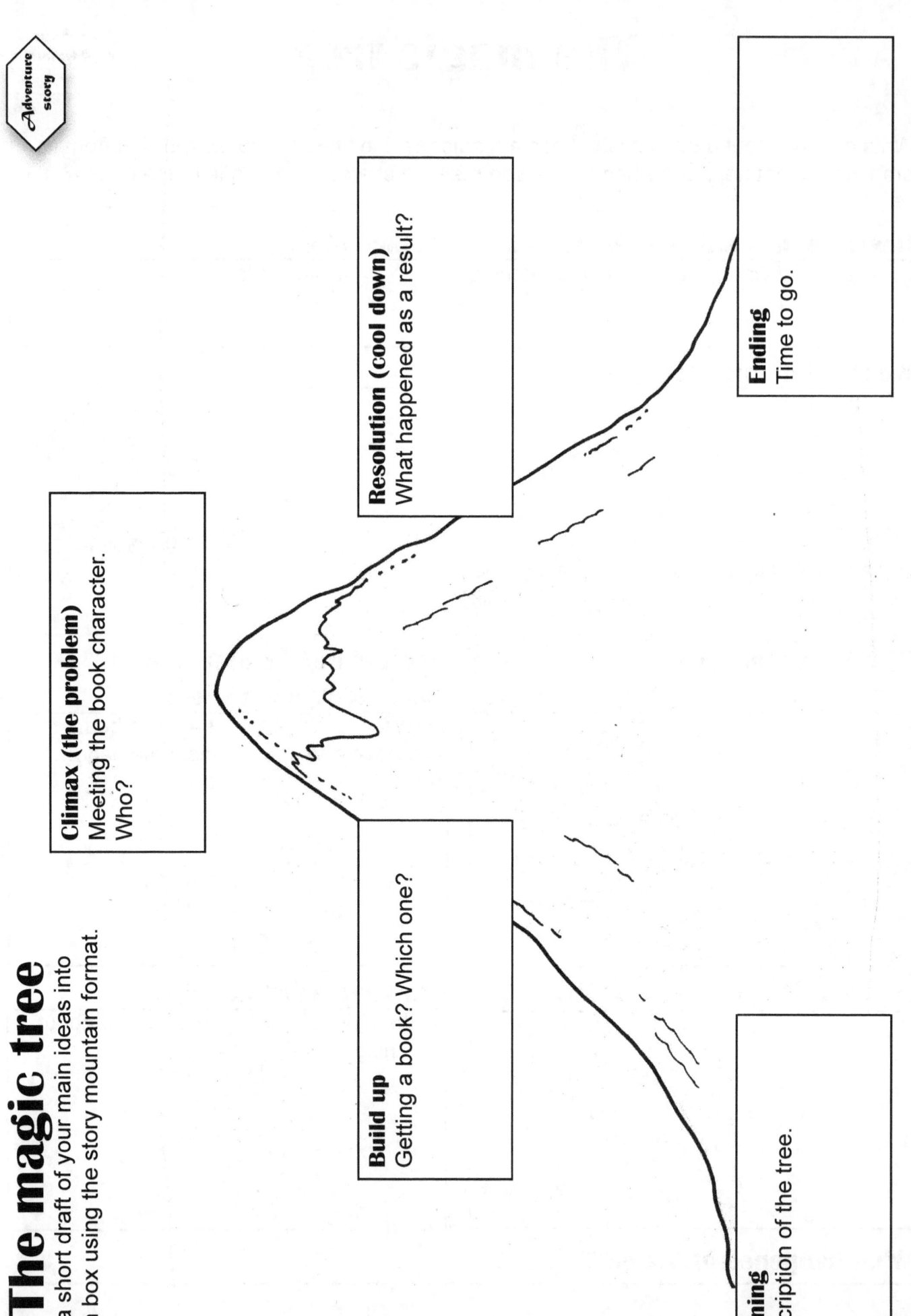

Wonderland

Write a descriptive account about a person who shrinks in size and then finds a little door which leads into an amazing garden.

Opening sentence

"Oh no! I have a really sharp pain," I said. Next minute I started to shrink. I felt most peculiar as I got smaller and smaller until I was the perfect size to go through the tiny door into the garden.

What is the weather like in the garden?

What is the first thing you see/hear in the garden? Then what?

What do you see, hear, small, taste, feel and do in this rather unusual garden? Build up your description step-by-step.

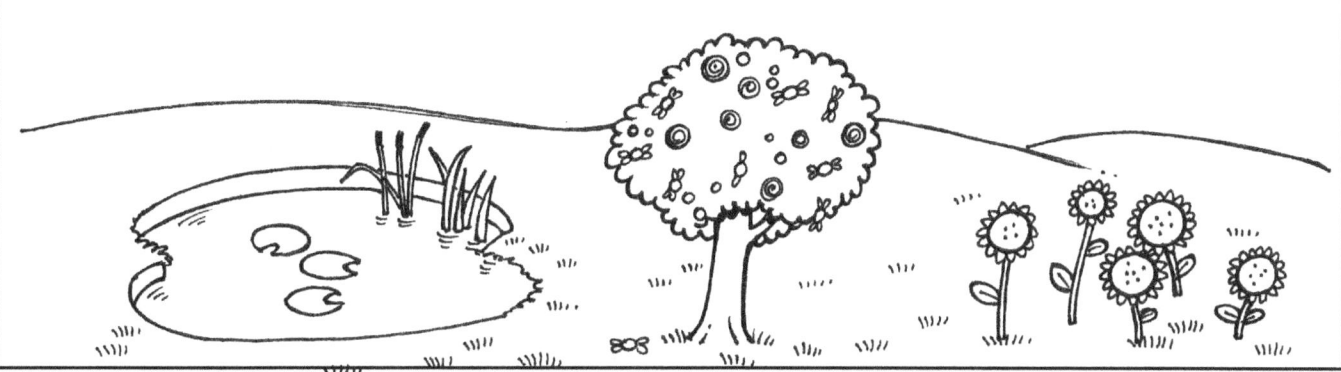

Who do you meet? Do they show you around the garden?

What do you do in the garden? Do you take away anything?

Boost Creative Writing, Years 3–4
© Judith Thornby and Brilliant Publications Limited

Wonderland

Draw, colour and label a mind map of ideas. Be descriptive!

What do you see/hear first?

What was the weather like?

What did you do next?

Who did you meet? Where did you go?

What did you see next?

The Very Important Person (VIP)

A VIP is coming to your school. How does the school prepare? Be imaginative!

Who? How was the exciting news told to the school?

Ideas: the Queen   a Member of Parliament   a pop star

How does the school prepare? What jobs need to be done?

Who? (Head teacher... cleaners... caretaker... pupils... cook) What do they have to do?

Ideas: caretaker is getting very flustered because...
The cleaners are scrubbing the...
The pupils in Class ____ are busy making...
The red carpets in the local shop have all sold out, so the head teacher has to...
Class ____ is finding out what the VIP's favourite food/colour is

On the big day

Ideas: Early morning preparations: balloons, bunting, banners, tables set with food
Red carpet rolled out
Arrival of the VIP... car?
Sitting down to eat... what happens?

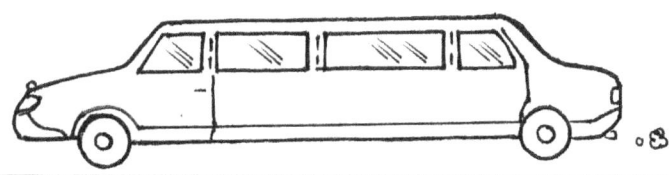

Afterwards

Ideas:
Does it all goes to plan?
How does the caretaker feel when it is all over?
What happens to the red carpet?
Do you get a thank you message or a gift from the VIP a few days later?

The Very Important Person (VIP)

Descriptive account

Draw, colour and label a mind map of ideas. Use powerful describing words!

How was the school getting ready? What was happening?

Ideas: paint cans, red carpet delivery van, bustle of maintenance staff

What was happening in the classes?
What were they making?

What was cooking in the school kitchen?
Food: colour, texture, smell, taste.

What was being cleaned/washed?
Cups, floors, door handles – add detailed description.

The lunch table – where?
What decorations were there?

Arrival of the VIP
How? car? carriage? plane?

A day on fantasy island

Write a story about a person who arrived at a fantasy island early one morning. There was a luxury house to stay in and amazing things to do.

How did the person get to the island?

Ideas: private jet   hot air balloon   boat

Where was the house? What was so special about it?

What could the person see? hear? smell? taste? How was the person feeling?
Ideas: an amazing bedroom? fantastic games room?
incredible chest full of interesting things – what?
a fantastic personal chef – what lovely things did he cook when the person arrived?

What things where there to do on the island?

Then what appeared on the island? Describe in detail.

Ideas: fun fair on a pier   aqua world   private zoo

What were the person's thoughts about the fantasy island at the end of the day?

Boost Creative Writing, Years 3–4
© Judith Thornby and Brilliant Publications Limited

Descriptive account

Bedroom in the fantasy island house

Draw, colour and label a mind map of ideas. Use powerful describing words!

What was the bed like?

What did you like best?

What toys were in the chest?
Describe the shape, colour, texture, movement.

Was there anybody else in the room?

What made the room really special?

Ideas: games room at one end of it

What did the chef bring you up to eat?

This page may be photocopied for use by the purchasing institution only.

The shop of magical things

Descriptive account

Write a descriptive story about someone who visits a shop which is full of magical things.

Where is it? What does the outside of the shop look like?

Add details!

Idea: lime green door with a beautiful silver door knob shaped like a dragon's head…

What do you see when the door opens?

Tucked away in the corner of the room…
On the ceiling…
On a huge shelf…

Ideas: huge basket of broomsticks   gigantic golden web   potion bottles

What do you see next? Then what happens?

In the middle of the room…

Ideas: enormous wardrobe   magic trainers   wizard's hat

Who is at the till? What do you buy? Then what do you do?

Boost Creative Writing, Years 3–4
© Judith Thornby and Brilliant Publications Limited

Descriptive account

The shop of magical things

Draw, colour and label a mind map of ideas. Use powerful describing words!

What did the outside of the shop look like?
Draw things in detail: handle, window, door, etc. Describe the colour, shape, texture, material (brass, silver…)

What did you see in the shop?
Describe shape, colour, texture, movement.

What did you hear? smell?

What did you see?

Who/what was behind the counter?

Camping out!

Ideas for an opening

It was the ideal place to camp…. We could see busy birds darting about high up in the branches. Smoke was wafting out of a nearby farmhouse chimney. The sun was sparkling and fluffy clouds were floating in the blue sky. We could hear the water rippling in a little stream and the leafy trees swishing gently in the warm breeze.

Setting – the perfect place to camp

What could we see? What could we hear?

Ideas: woods   field   beach   garden

What did we do at the camp?

Ideas:
pitched the tent, gathered… (twigs for a fire)
collected…(blackberries, conkers)
lit the campfire/barbecue… sizzled sausages
snuggled down in our sleeping bags at sunset

In the middle of the night

We instantly fell asleep but something awoke us in the middle of the night.
What could we hear? How did it make us feel?

Ideas:
scuffling noise… pair of eyes stared at us (was it an animal – what kind?) – Next?
rumbling sound… bolt of lightning, poured with rain, tent leaking – Next?
moaning noise… whistling wind, branches rustled, tree creaked – Next?

Ending

Idea:
In the morning we had a good laugh about our adventure in the night. We could not wait to tell our family what had happened.

Descriptive account

Camping out!

Possible WOW words
Use powerful verbs and amazing adjectives.

Amazing adjectives		Powerful verbs	
tall magnificent	trees	swayed shivered	in the wind
crunchy	leaves	rustled	underfoot
soft freshly cut cushiony velvety	grass		
cool fresh	water	rippled splashed	in the stream/river/pond
busy	squirrels hedgehogs	darted about snuffled around	
warm	sun	sparkled glinted	
fluffy cotton wool	clouds	glided floated	

Amazing adjectives		Powerful verbs	
	fire	crackled sputtered	
	sausages	sizzled hissed	
	baked beans	bubbled	in a pot
delicious tasty	smell	wafted drifted	across
creamy scrumptious chocolate	cake/cookies		
	stars	gleamed glowed	in the night sky
		snuggled	down
cosy warm	sleeping bag		
scraping rustling pattering	sound		

Suddenly... Next minute...

Amazing adjectives		Powerful verbs	
stripy shadowy furry/hairy	face	peered	in
startled black beady huge yellow	eyes	watched gazed stared	
	rain	pelted poured	down
	bolts of lightning	rumbled flashed streaked	across
		scrambled	out of the tent
		rushed raced	inside the...
		dripping	wet

It was so... scary... funny.

A visit to the dentist

Write a descriptive account of a visit to the dentist.

Opening sentences
How are you feeling as you walk through the door? Create a tense atmosphere.

Describe the waiting room
What can you see?
What can you hear?
What can you smell?
How are you feeling?
What do you do while you are waiting?

Ideas: quiet, chatter, full, empty, goldfish, magazines, screech of drill, ticking of clock, smell of disinfectant, worried, confident

In with the dentist
What is the dentist like? What is the room like?

What does the dentist say and do?
Do you have any treatment? What happens next? Describe step-by-step.

Final thoughts
How are you feeling now the visit is over? Do you feel a lot better?

A visit to the dentist

Descriptive account

Draw, colour and label a mind map of ideas. Use powerful describing words!

Describe the waiting room
What can you see? hear? smell? How are you feeling?

How do you feel when you walk in the door?

What does the dentist say or do?

What is the room like?

What is the dentist like?

The enchanted water

Write a traditional tale about what happened when some enchanted water appeared in the kingdom!

Format
✻ Opening (Once upon a time…)
✻ Setting
✻ Characters (the goodie and the baddie)
✻ Problem/trouble
✻ Good character saves the day
✻ Ending (…all lived happily ever after)

Setting	Character (baddie)	Character (goodie)
witch's cottage	goblin	elf
magician's castle	witch	pixie
wizard's cave	wizard	any person
palace gardens		
woods		

Trouble (build up to the climax or exciting part of the story)

What water did the Baddie make enchanted? Where was it?
What happened as a result of the trouble?

Ideas:

A swim in a pool makes someone grow a fish tail	At first better at swimming but then fish tail uncomfortable
A drink of water from a well gives someone webbed feet like a duck	could not wear any shoes and feet got very sore

Who saved the day? How?

Ending

The enchanted water – vocabulary

Story opener

Once upon a time…

Long, long ago…

In a faraway land…

A long time ago…

Middle sections (build up, climax, resolution)

That very morning…

On his/her way…

It wasn't long before…

Suddenly…

But as soon as…

A split second later…

Shortly afterwards

Everybody tried to help…

Nothing worked until one day…

Ending

He/she lived happily ever after.

He/she decided never to…

And nothing was heard of the ……………

ever again!

More vocabulary

The magic potion gleamed in the pot

…poured the mixture carefully into a little bottle

…waited until there was no one around

…tipped it quickly into the…

…watched as ……………… jumped into the pool/drank the water from the well

The enchanted water

Put a short draft of your main ideas into each box using the story mountain format.

Traditional tale

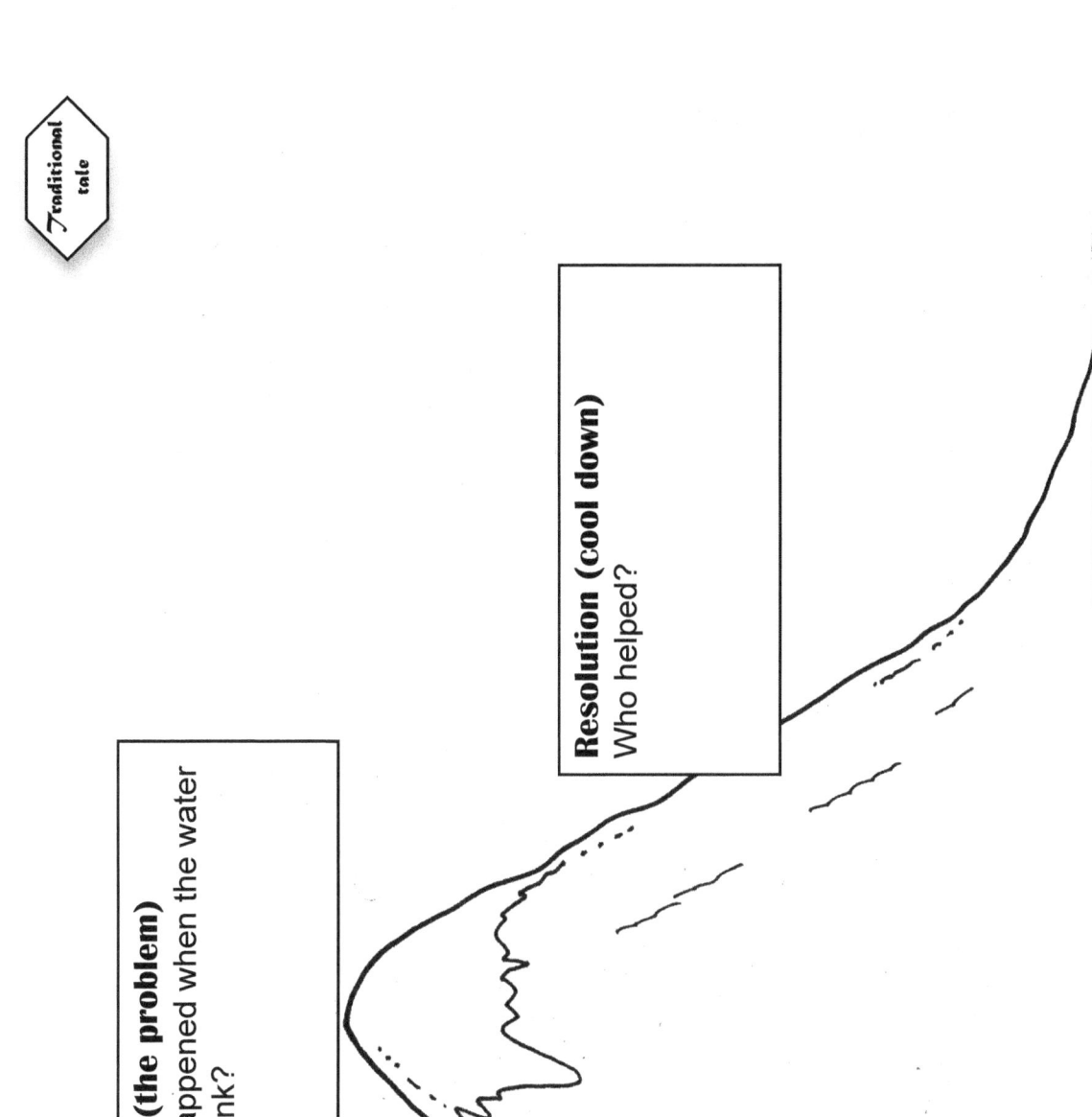

Climax (the problem)
What happened when the water was drunk?

Resolution (cool down)
Who helped?

Ending
What happens?

Build up
How did the water become enchanted?

Opening
Describe the main character and setting.

Boost Creative Writing, Years 3–4
© Judith Thornby and Brilliant Publications Limited

This page may be photocopied for use by the purchasing institution only.

My mythical creature

Draw and label a picture of your mythical creature.

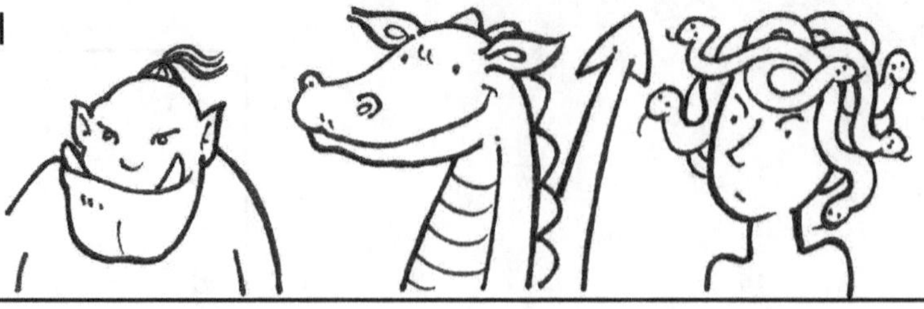

Name of creature:

Ideas: size? shape? skin covering? colour?

body	eyes	snout	fangs	tentacles	hair
webbed feet	claws	horn	scales	wings	tail
spotted	striped	hairy	spiky	pointed	smooth
legs					

My mythical creature

What did it look like? (Look at your picture!)
Add detail

Ideas:

size	It was a massive fearsome beast
body	(body of a snake and the head of a…)
claws	(sharp, pointed)
feet	(webbed, stubby)
tails	(spiky, long)
wings	(huge, bony)
covered in	(glittering scales, thick fur)

Use similes:
It had curved fangs like sharp razors
…eyes like sharp daggers
Its eyes glowed like…

What did it smell like?

Ideas:
It smelt like it had been sleeping in a rubbish dump with disgusting rotten…
and mouldy old…

What noise did it make if it was angry?

Ideas:
It bellowed like a bull when he was…
It howled like a…
It roared like a…

The noise could be heard for…
(what distance away?)

Where did it live?

Ideas:
swamp
marsh
middle of a maze
dark cave

What special power did it have?

Ideas:
It breathed out fireballs from its mouth
It could turn people into stone with its laser eyes.

Boost Creative Writing, Years 3–4
© Judith Thornby and Brilliant Publications Limited

 fable/myth

My myth

Many years ago when the world was young there lived a fearsome creature called the ....

The mythical creature
Description of the fantastical beast (look at your picture).

What has the creature done to cause upset?
Ideas:
turned 20 people in to stone
kidnapped a beautiful girl
eaten all the cows and goats in the land

The hero
A brave young man called .... decided to defeat the monster, but he did not know how, so he decided to go to Mount Olympus to get help from ....

Ideas: Zeus   Apollo   Athena   Hera   Artemis   Ares

Gifts to help the hero

winged sandals
to travel more easily

magical dagger
to kill the creature

enchanted shield
protection from creature's blows

charmed mirror
if the creature saw its reflection it would die

The journey and the struggle with the beast
Ideas:
He travelled over/across .... for several days until he arrived at the .... where the monster lived. It was a fierce struggle…

The ending
Ideas:
.... was rewarded for his bravery and given lots of .... for slaying the monstrous creature.

One good turn deserves another

Write a short story involving two animals that teaches a lesson or a moral. This kind of story is called a fable.

Animal 1 (Describe looks/character)	**Animal 2** (Describe looks/character)

Setting?
Add detail.

Ideas:
in the jungle   by a river bank   in the wood

How does Animal 1 get in trouble? How does Animal 2 help?
Describe step by step.

A few days later…

Ideas:
stuck in a net trap   huge thorn in paw   caught in a forest fire   poorly – unable to get food to eat

How does Animal 2 get in trouble? How does Animal 1 help?
Soon after…

The moral of the story is…

Granny – a rhyming poem

Write a funny rhyming poem. Create a pretend conversation between a child and a granny who is deaf.

For example:
Amy: Shall I close the gate?
Granny: I do not think you are late.

Amy: Be careful not to stumble.
Granny: Yes I do like apple crumble.

Amy: Would you like anything from town?
Granny: No, I cannot see a clown.

Amy: Are you feeling a bit sick?
Granny: No, thank you, I don't need my stick.

Amy: Have I got a spot on my face?
Granny: Oh no, I don't think I could win a race.

Start by working out words with the same rhyming patterns. Then think of your sentences. Here are a few to start you off:

ate	crate gate late mate plate slate
umble	crumble grumble jumble mumble stumble
ink	drink pink rink sink think wink
ell	bell sell shell smell spell well yell
ace	brace face lace place race trace

Rhyming ideas:
ain   ack   atch   ight   ice   eat   udge   ake   ound

Granny – a rhyming poem

by ....

.... : ....

Granny: ....

.... : ....

Granny: ....

.... : ....

Granny: ....

.... : ....

Granny: ....

.... : ....

Granny: ....

A haiku riddle

A haiku is a Japanese poem about nature, but you can choose any topic. It is a three line syllable poem. Create and illustrate your own haikus.

Example: Line 1   Rolled up on a plate   **5** syllables
          Line 2   Oozing with maple syrup   **7** syllables
          Line 3   Delicious to eat   **5** syllables

Winter

Pick a wintry word from the ideas sheet. Play around with WOW words to make poetic lines. Choose one line to be the repeating line in your poem.

Wintry words	WOW words
night	Cold dark **nights** stretch out

Repeating line:

Winter – ideas sheet

Wintry words		WOW words
evenings nights trees	long dark bare leafless	stretch out
hands teeth	chilly chattering	shivering cold
pavements ponds slopes	slippery icy frozen	slide skid slip skate ski
frost icicles snowflakes	sparkling silvery	twinkles glitters hang float
gloves scarves fire	warm cosy crackling	wrap up snuggle down curl up
cocoa soup	delicious tasty	steaming hot
cinnamon sticks candles	spicy sweet smelling	glow
robin owl pheasants	friendly flat faced long tailed	looks for stares struts
holly berries	prickly	grow

Keep the rhythm of the poem. Think of a repeating line!

Idea:
Slippery pavements
Icy slopes
Fun to ski down
Winter is here

A seasonal letter

Write a chatty letter from Mr Winter to Miss Spring, telling her news about the season of winter and what he is looking forward to in spring.

Mr Winter's address (make it sound winter-like: Snowball Cottage, Holly Lane, The Wood)

....
....
....
....

Dear Miss Spring,
I have been meaning to write to you for a while. I hope you are keeping well…

Chatty bits of news

Ideas:
skiing, sledging, building snowmen, new warm furry boots, cuddled up in front of a hot fire, Christmas dinner, frost, icicles, snow, bleak bare trees

What is Mr Winter looking forward to when Miss Spring arrives

Ideas:
getting out in the garden, blossom, shoots, greenery, leaves, nests, chicks, lambs, tadpoles, cutting grass, lighter evenings, bulbs, daffodils, bluebells

Questions Mr Winter might ask Miss Spring

Have you…?
Are you…?
I wonder if…?

Ending sentence
I hope you will write back to me soon.

Love from,

.... Mr Winter

A chatty letter

Write a letter to a friend, relation or pen pal telling them all your news.

Your address

....
....
....
....

Dear…
How are you? I thought I would write you a letter to…

Chatty bits of news

Ideas:
outings?
school events?
home news?

What are you really looking forward to?

Idea:
going on holiday

Ask questions

Have you…?
Are you…?
I wonder if…?

Ending sentence
I hope you will write back to me soon.

Love from,

....

This page may be photocopied for use by the purchasing institution only.
56

Boost Creative Writing, Years 3–4
© Judith Thornby and Brilliant Publications Limited

A letter to an author

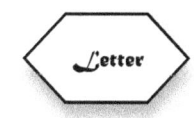

Write a letter to your favourite author, inviting them to your school's book week. Don't forget to use paragraphs.

Your address

....
....
....
....

Date

Dear...
(Mr, Miss, Mrs, Ms)

Tell the author the reason you are writing the letter.

Ideas:
I am inviting you to visit…
Tell the author what activities the school does during book week.

Tell the author something about yourself

Ideas:
age? class? interests?

Tell the author which of his/her books you have liked and why.
Ask the author some questions

Where did you get the idea…?
Have you…?
I wonder if…?

Ending sentence
I do hope that you will write back to me to say that you can come to the school.

Yours sincerely,

....

Boost Creative Writing, Years 3–4
© Judith Thornby and Brilliant Publications Limited

Book review

Title:

Author:

What was the story about?

Who was your favourite character and why?

Which part of the story did you like best?

Who would like this story?

How many stars would you give this book?

☆ ☆ ☆ ☆ ☆

My favourite pet animal

Plan an information report about a type of pet.

- Introduction
- Behaviour/'talk'
- Keeping clean and healthy/grooming
- Fun and games/exercise
- Breeds
- Did you know? Interesting facts
- Feeding time What? How much?

My animal report

Don't forget to make it interesting!
Headings
Pictures and diagrams
Label different bits
Fun features: facts in paw prints, thought bubbles

Boost Creative Writing, Years 3–4
© Judith Thornby and Brilliant Publications Limited

My favourite pet animal

Plan an information report about a type of pet

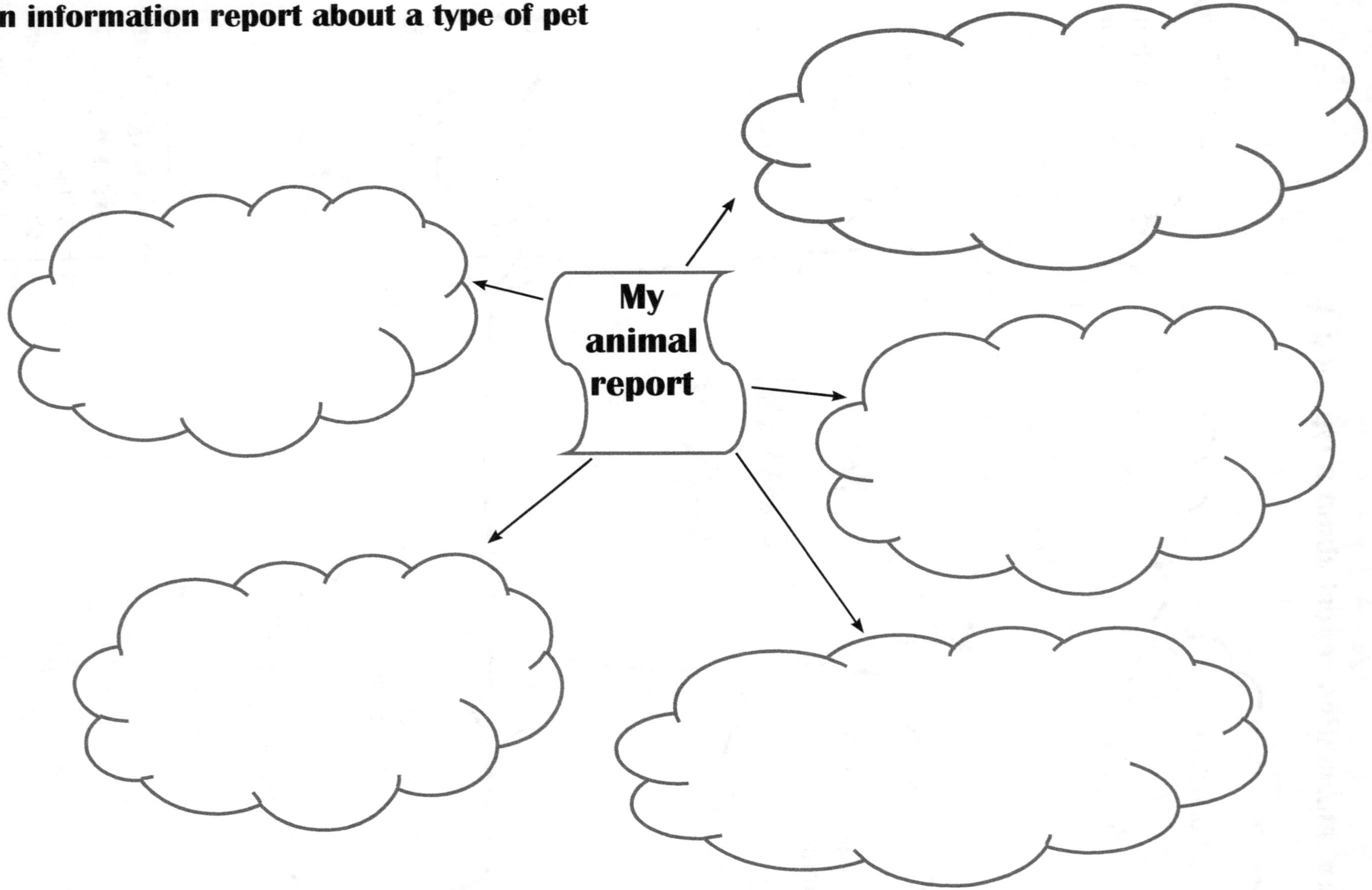

My animal report

The Ancient Greeks

Plan an information report about the influence and achievements of Ancient Greece. Use your ideas to create a non-chronological report.

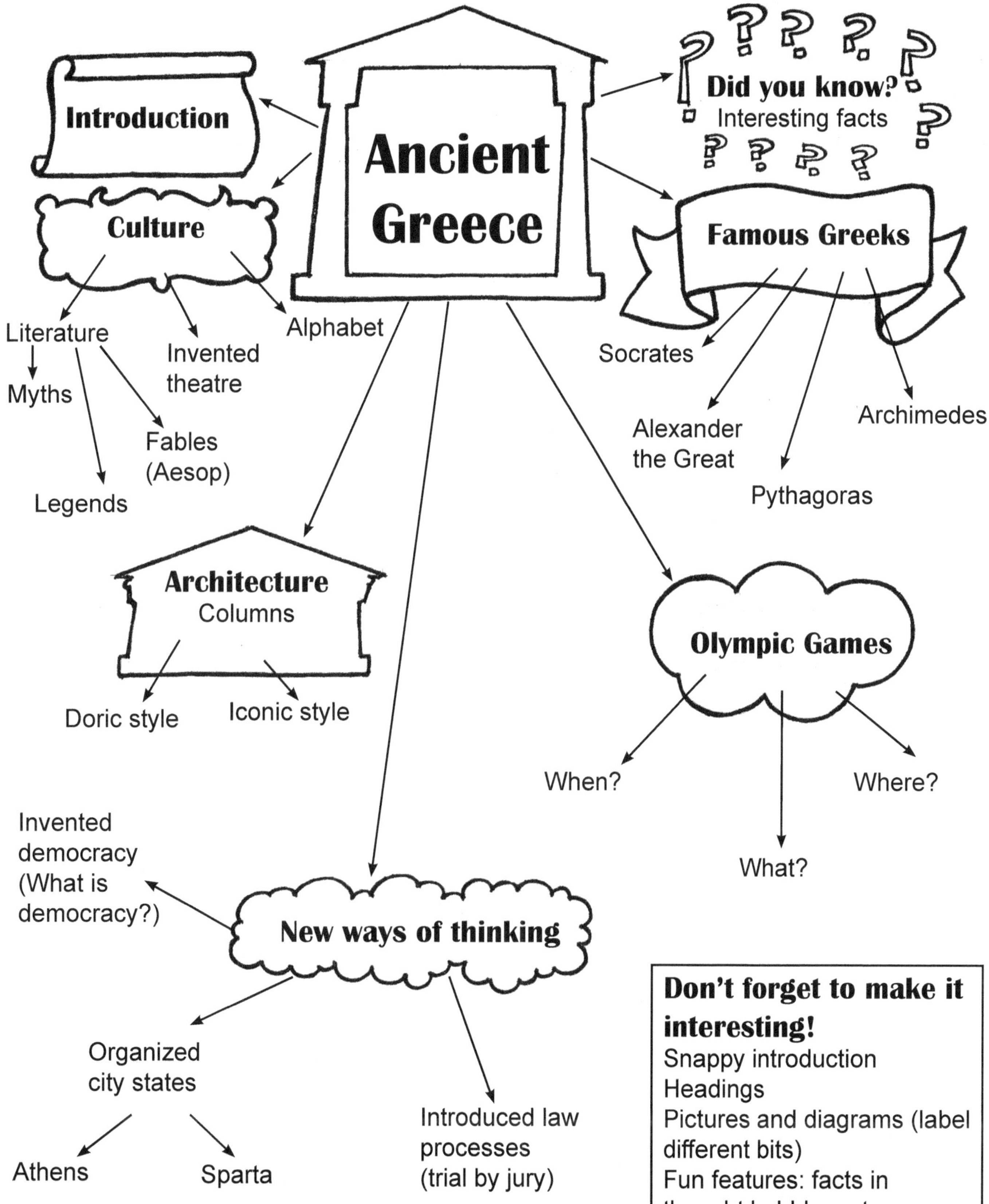

Ancient Greece (central topic) branches to:

- **Introduction**
- **Culture**
  - Literature → Myths → Legends
  - Invented theatre
  - Fables (Aesop)
  - Alphabet
- **Did you know?** Interesting facts
- **Famous Greeks**
  - Socrates
  - Alexander the Great
  - Pythagoras
  - Archimedes
- **Architecture** – Columns
  - Doric style
  - Iconic style
- **Olympic Games**
  - When?
  - What?
  - Where?
- **New ways of thinking**
  - Invented democracy (What is democracy?)
  - Organized city states
    - Athens
    - Sparta
  - Introduced law processes (trial by jury)

Don't forget to make it interesting!
- Snappy introduction
- Headings
- Pictures and diagrams (label different bits)
- Fun features: facts in thought bubbles, etc.

Iron Age Celts

Plan an information report about life in Iron Age Britain. Use your ideas to create a non-chronological report.

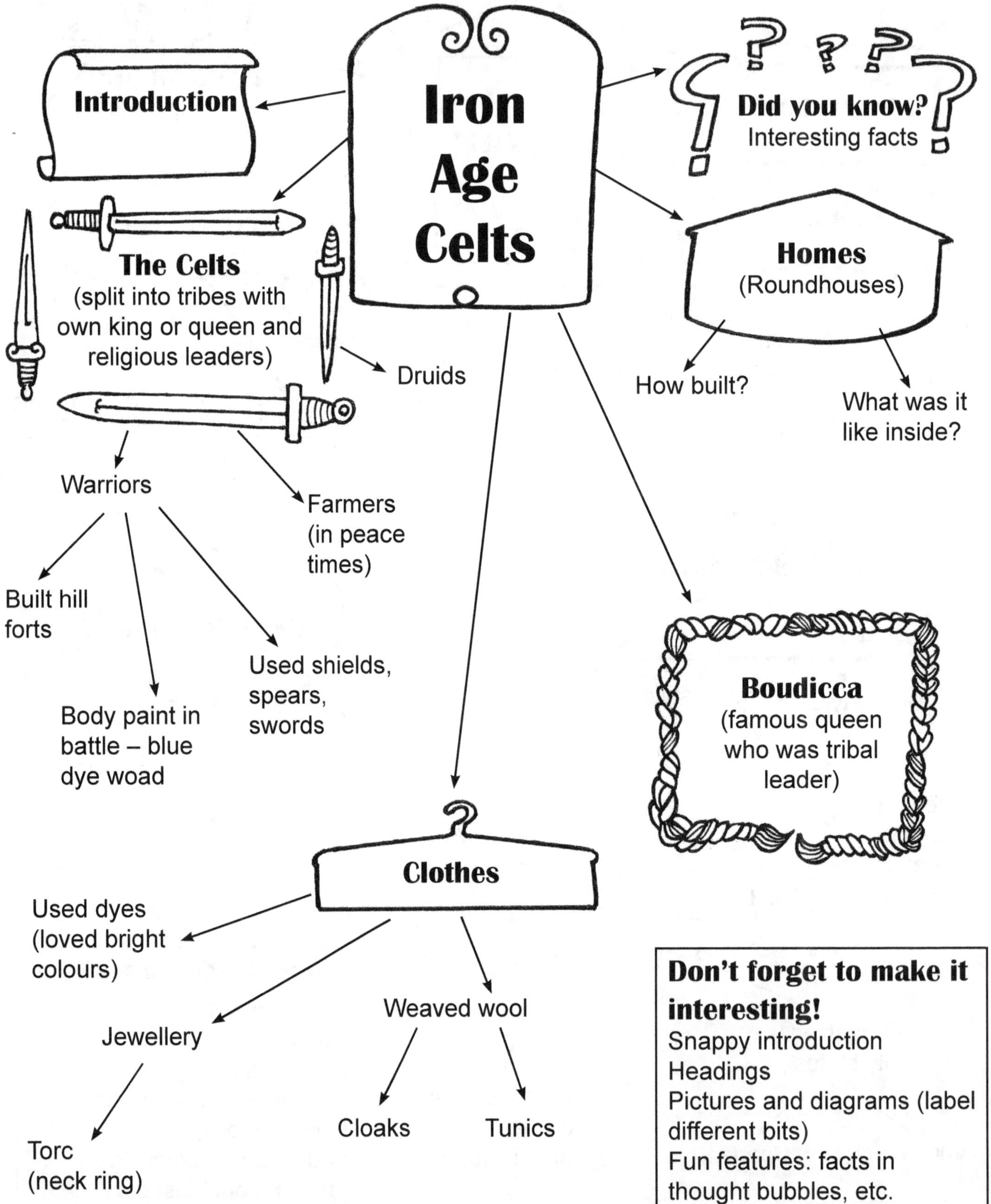

Iron Age Celts

- **Introduction**
- **Did you know?** Interesting facts
- **Homes** (Roundhouses)
  - How built?
  - What was it like inside?
- **The Celts** (split into tribes with own king or queen and religious leaders)
  - Druids
  - Farmers (in peace times)
  - Warriors
    - Built hill forts
    - Body paint in battle – blue dye woad
    - Used shields, spears, swords
- **Boudicca** (famous queen who was tribal leader)
- **Clothes**
  - Used dyes (loved bright colours)
  - Jewellery
    - Torc (neck ring)
  - Weaved wool
    - Cloaks
    - Tunics

Don't forget to make it interesting!
Snappy introduction
Headings
Pictures and diagrams (label different bits)
Fun features: facts in thought bubbles, etc.

My newspaper report

Write a **different version** of the story of Red Riding Hood as a newspaper report. Change the story so that the Wolf is the Goodie and Red Riding Hood is the Baddie.

Headline: Grab the reader's attention – make it interesting!

Idea: **Wolf only trying to help!**

Report the facts
Remember, in your version Red Riding Hood is the Baddie and the Wolf is the Goodie.

Answer the questions:
* Where did Red Riding Hood live?
* What was not very nice about her character? Why?
* What was she told to do?
* Where did the Wolf see her? Why did he follow her?
* How did he lose sight of her?
* What made the Wolf stop at Granny's house? Why was Granny upset?
* Why did the Wolf go into Granny's house? How did he help Granny?
* When Red Riding Hood arrived, what did she do to upset Granny?
* Why did the Wolf chase Red Riding Hood?

Reported by ....

For... (name of newspaper)

Use quotes
Ideas: What did the woodcutter say when he arrived?
I spoke to the woodcutter and he said that…

Vocabulary
cottage, woods, selfish, spoilt, cross, temper, tantrum, mother, asked, take, cupcakes, dropped, disappeared, passed, saw, helped, rude, only, wanted, teach her a lesson

My newspaper report

Reporter:

How to make pancakes

The pancake instructions are all mixed up. Can you put them in the correct order? The ingredients should be in the order they are used in the recipe.

What to do	You will need
Crack an egg into bowl.	an egg
Place on a plate and enjoy with sugar and lemon.	cup of milk
Whisk batter until smooth.	cup of flour
Cook for a minute and flip over; fry until golden.	knob of butter
Add flour and milk to the egg to make a batter.	frying pan
Spoon ½ small cup of batter into the pan.	sugar
Melt a knob of butter in the frying pan.	lemon

Boost Creative Writing, Years 3–4
© Judith Thornby and Brilliant Publications Limited

Make a super sandwich

Write instructions for making a super sandwich.

Bossy words (imperative words)

Get	Squeeze
Spread	Place
Add	Press (together)
Slice	Cut (in half)
Chop	Eat
Grate	Enjoy
Sprinkle	

More vocabulary

brown bread, butter, margarine, cream cheese, cheese, ham, chicken, lettuce, cucumber, crisps, jelly, tomato ketchup, brown sauce, salad cream, pieces, slices, knife, plate

The clever trick

The Enormous Crocodile was cross with the Roly Poly bird for spoiling his trick. He waddled off into the jungle to think of another plan.

A little while later... where did he play his next trick?
Ideas:

at the funfair   at the school   in the jungle

What did he pretend to be? How did he disguise himself?

Ideas:
cuddly crocodile prize at the fun fair ... which stall?
orange tree
bookshelf at school

What did the children do?

Who warned the children? How?
Remember to use speech marks and start a new line for each new speaker.

Ideas:
Humpy Rumpy the elephant, Trunky the elephant, Muggle Wump the monkey

How did the Enormous Crocodile feel?
Did he wonder what he could do for his next trick?

Vocabulary: absolutely furious, a great big sulk

The clever trick

Plan another clever trick that the Clever Crocodile might play using the story mountain format.

Roald Dahl

Climax (the problem)
What did Crocodile try to do?

Resolution (cool down)
Who ruined the plan?

Build up
Planning the trick.

Opening
Describe the setting. What could you see? hear?

Ending
How did Crocodile feel?

Mr Twit's trick

What does Mr Twit look like?
Draw and label a picture of Mr Twit. Use powerful adjectives to describe him.

Vocabulary
beard, eyebrows, face, bristles, nostrils, ear holes, tufts of hair, tongue, thick, spiky, dirty, smelly, mouldy, foul, revolting, horrible, disgusting

Mr Twit's trick

Put a short draft of your main ideas into each box using the story mountain format.

Climax (the problem)
Playing the trick.

Resolution (cool down)
Results of the trick.

Build up
Planning the trick.

Ending
Promise of revenge.

Opening
Describe Mr Twit's character (look at your picture to help).

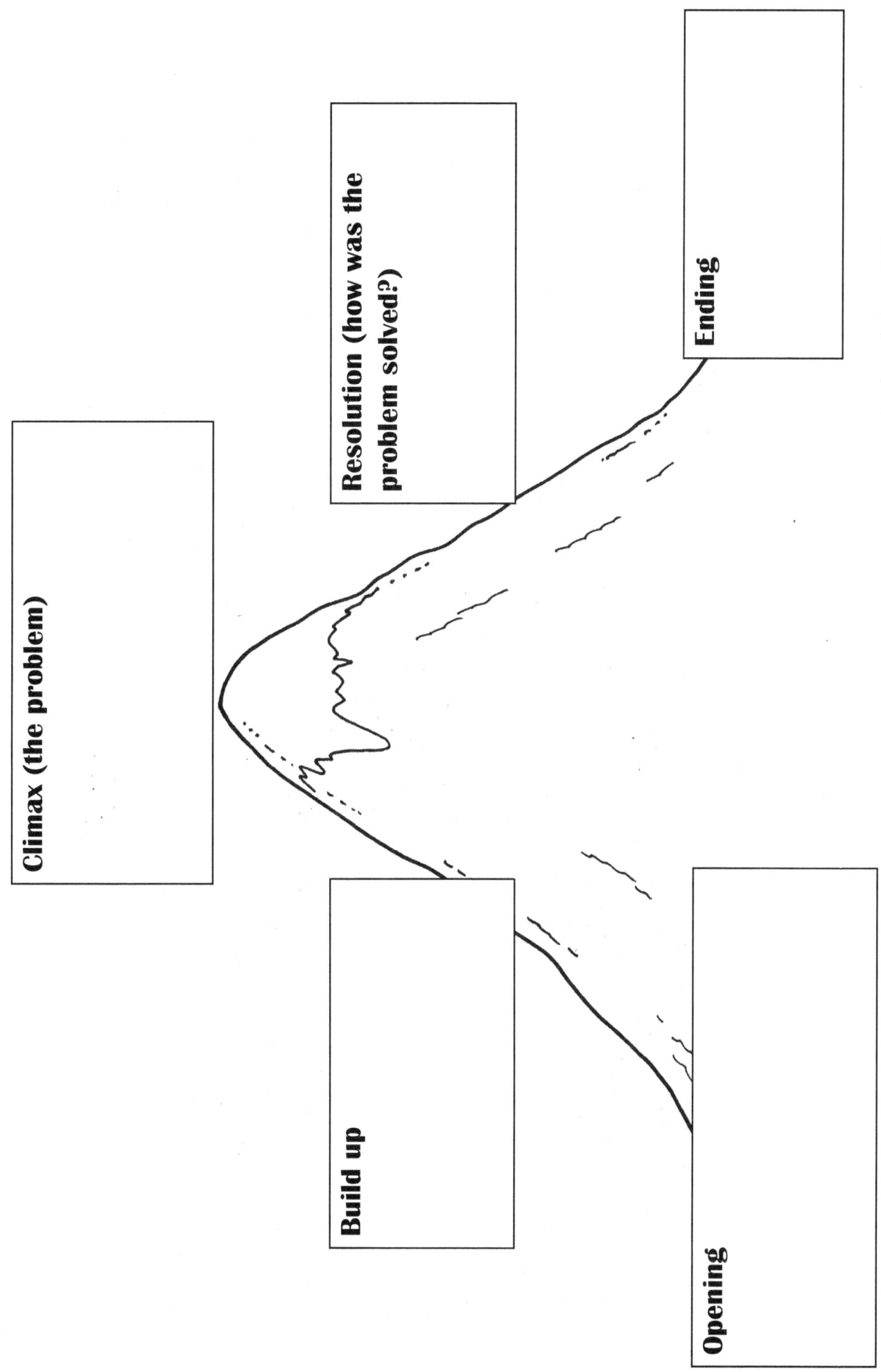

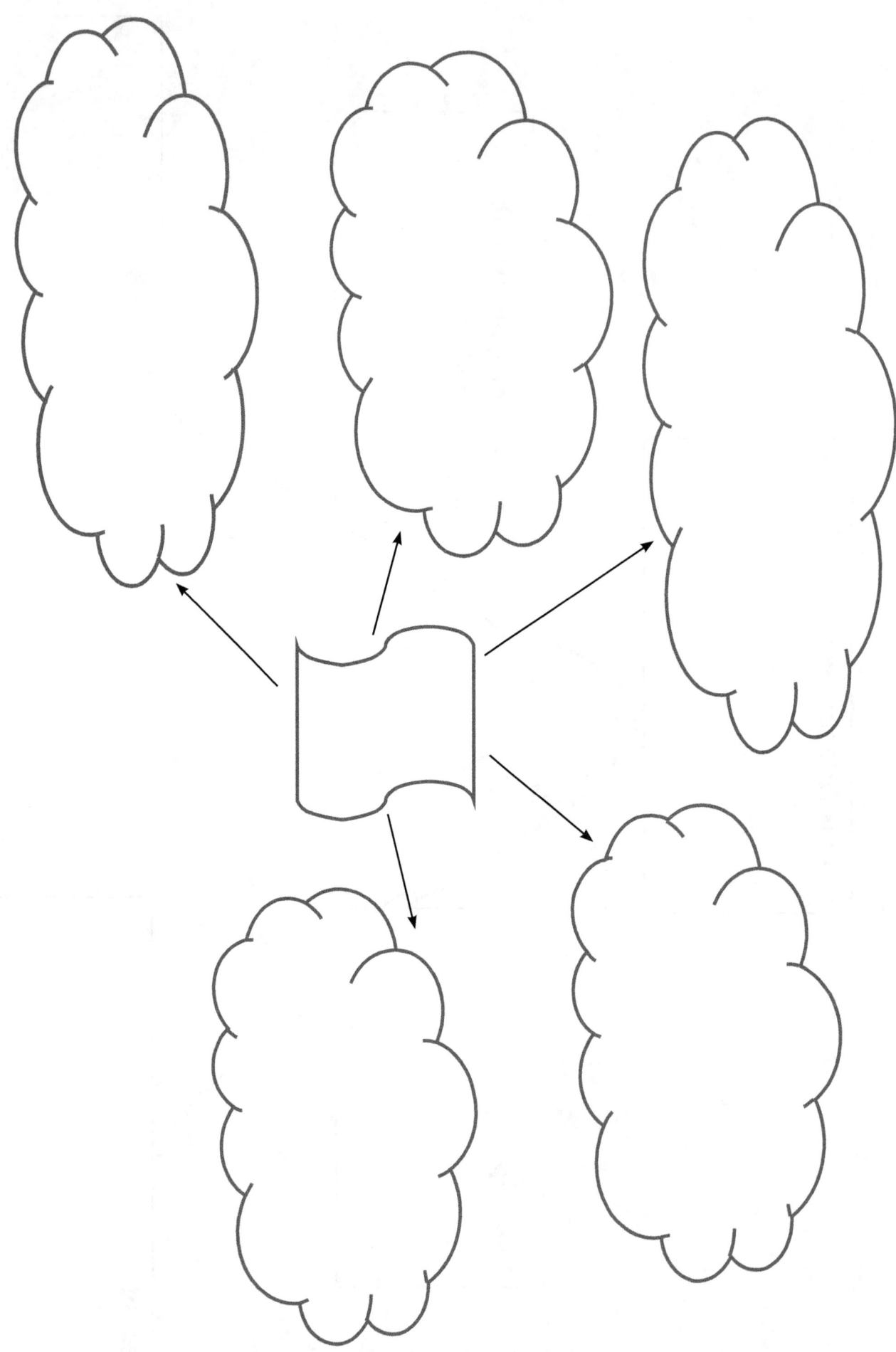

Ages: 9–11yrs

Boost Creative Writing
Planning Sheets to Support Writers (Especially SEN Pupils) in Years 5–6

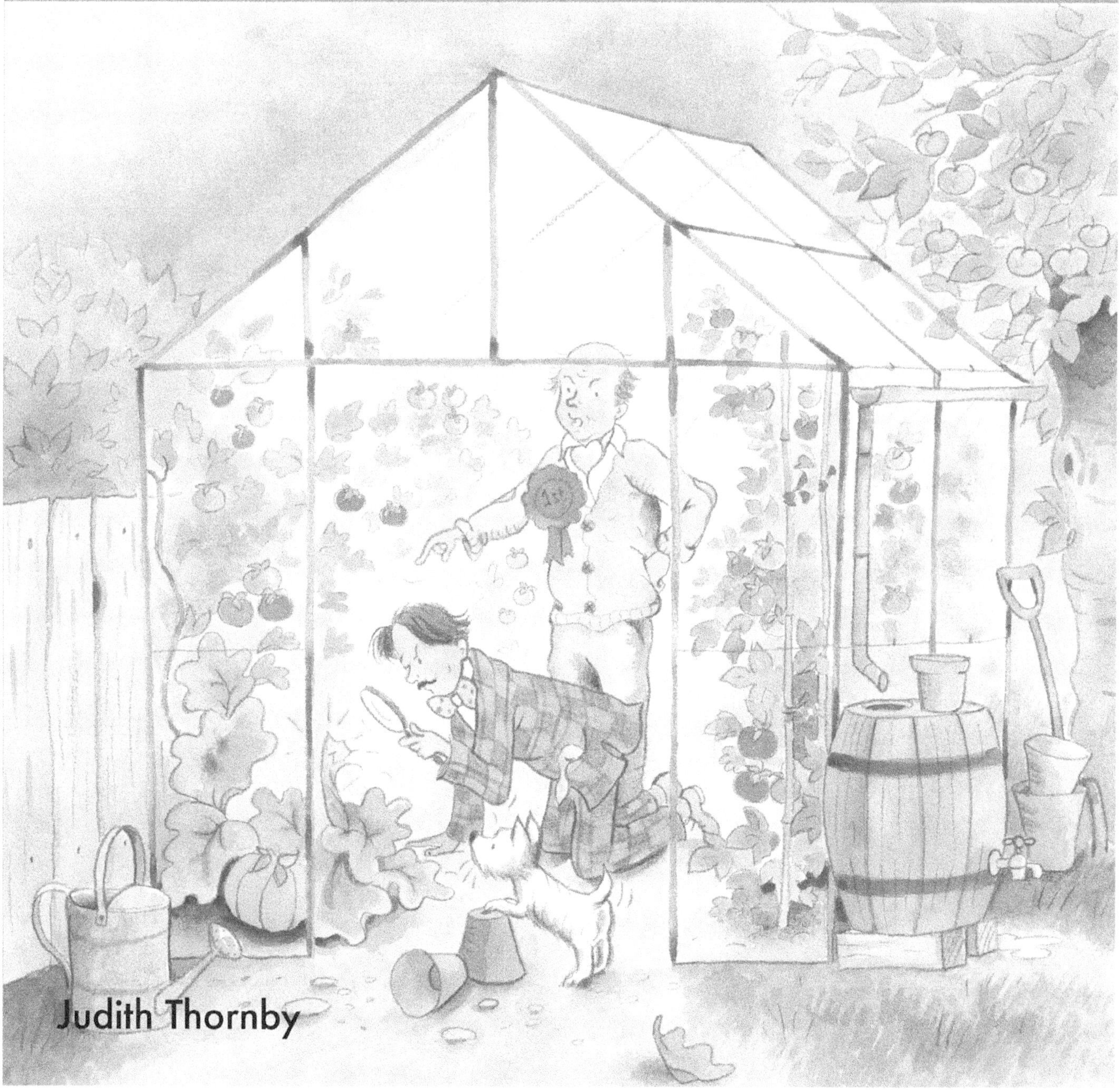

Judith Thornby

Boost Creative Writing

Planning Sheets to Support Writers (Especially SEN Pupils) in Years 5-6

Judith Thornby

We hope you and your pupils enjoy using the ideas in this book. Brilliant Publications publishes many other books to help primary school teachers. To find out more details on all of our titles, including those listed below, please go to our website: www.brilliantpublications.co.uk.

Boost Creative Writing – Years 1–2	978-1-78317-058-6
Boost Creative Writing – Years 3–4	978-1-78317-059-3
Brilliant Activities for Reading Comprehension, Year 1	978-1-78317-070-8
Brilliant Activities for Reading Comprehension, Year 2	978-1-78317-071-5
Brilliant Activities for Reading Comprehension, Year 3	978-1-78317-072-2
Brilliant Activities for Reading Comprehension, Year 4	978-1-78317-073-9
Brilliant Activities for Reading Comprehension, Year 5	978-1-78317-074-6
Brilliant Activities for Reading Comprehension, Year 6	978-1-78317-075-3
Brilliant Activities for Creative Writing, Year 1	978-0-85747-463-6
Brilliant Activities for Creative Writing, Year 2	978-0-85747-464-3
Brilliant Activities for Creative Writing, Year 3	978-0-85747-465-0
Brilliant Activities for Creative Writing, Year 4	978-0-85747-466-7
Brilliant Activities for Creative Writing, Year 5	978-0-85747-467-4
Brilliant Activities for Creative Writing, Year 6	978-0-85747-468-1
Developing Reading Comprehension Skills Years 5-6: Classic Children's Literature	978-0-85747-837-5
Developing Reading Comprehension Skills Years 5-6: Classic Poetry	978-0-85747-846-7
How to Achieve Outstanding Writers in the EYFS and KS1	978-0-85747-838-2
Cracking Creative Writing	978-0-85747-831-3
Boost Spelling Skills	978-0-85747-803-0

Published by Brilliant Publications Limited
Unit 10
Sparrow Hall Farm
Edlesborough
Dunstable
Bedfordshire
LU6 2ES, UK

www.brilliantpublications.co.uk

The name Brilliant Publications and the logo are registered trademarks.

Written by Judith Thornby
Illustrated by Chantal Kees
Cover illustration by Frank Endersby
Designed by Brilliant Publications Limited

© Text Judith Thornby 2014
© Design Brilliant Publications Limited 2014

Printed book ISBN: 978-1-78317-060-9
E-book ISBN: 978-1-78317-063-0

First printed and published in the UK in 2014

The right of Judith Thornby to be identified as the author of this work has been asserted by herself in accordance with the Copyright, Designs and Patents Act 1988.

Pages 6–66 may be photocopied by individual teachers acting on behalf of the purchasing institution for classroom use only, without permission from the publisher and without declaration to the Copyright Licensing Agency or Publishers' Licensing Services. The materials may not be reproduced in any other form or for any other purpose without the prior permission of the publisher.

Contents

Introduction   4
Links to the National Curriculum   5
Suggested writing targets   6
Editing checklists   7–9

Tips for writing booklet   10–19

Adventure story
Amusing animal adventure story   20
The secret in the attic   21
The unwelcome animal visitor
  in the night   22–23
A spooky tale   24
The strange encounter in the school
  library   25–26
A scary story   27–28

Fantasy
The bubble that manages to break
  free and escape   29
First person fantasy story   30

Descriptive account
A descriptive account of a beach   31–32
A day in your life which you remember
  well   33
Rescue from the Titanic   34–35

Report/recount
Dear Diary   36
My newspaper report   37–38
A day in the sweatshop   39–40

Persuasive
What snacks should be allowed in
  school?   41
Article for the Nursery Rhyme Gazette   42
Be an eco-school – design a poster   43

Mystery story
A mystery story – whodunnit?   44
Whodunnit – structure   45
Whodunnit – report by detective   46
Whodunnits – vocabulary used   47
The case of the missing prize pumpkin   48

Poetry
Poem about a rainforest animal or plant   49–51
A simile poem   52–53

Play script
Battle of Hastings 1066 (a play script)   54–55
Conversations overheard   56–57

Shakespeare
William Shakespeare –
  my autobiography   58–59
Macbeth   60–62
Midsummer Night's Dream   63

Templates
Story mountain template   64
Mind map template   65
Bring in the senses   66

Introduction

These series of planning sheets aim to provide a structured resource which gives plenty of scope for exploring and collecting ideas in the different writing genres: adventure, fantasy, recount, letter, poetry etc. They generate discussion within a defined framework and then aid pupils to write more descriptive stories and compose longer pieces of writing.

Reluctant writers or those writers who struggle with the organization of their ideas can express themselves with more self-assurance by using these planning sheets. Confident writers can also benefit by delving into them to gain further ideas.

Some sheets can be written on directly but many are designed as a prop to refer to when writing. Vocabulary sheets are incorporated with some stories to help the flow of ideas.

Story mountain and mind map templates are included to assist narrative and descriptive writing and to cater for different learning styles. Visual learners have lots of imaginative ideas but might struggle with the sequence of events or the bare skeleton of the story so can benefit from using the story mountain approach. Logical systematic learners can sequence ideas but might struggle to develop them creatively and can benefit from using the mind map templates to expand descriptive writing.

I have specialized in the field of learning support since 1997 when I gained a diploma in specific learning difficulties. I am especially interested in promoting creative writing skills with children who are reluctant writers or who struggle with the organization of their ideas. These series of planning sheets generate discussion and aid in structuring composition in the different writing genres. They also can be used to give further ideas to confident writers as well. I have found that they have been successful in giving pupils greater self-assurance to express themselves in written form and have helped to make writing an enjoyable experience!

On page 5 you will see how the activities in the book link to the 2014 National Curriculum for England. On page 6 there are suggested writing targets. The way I use these is to cut out the relevant one(s) and tape them to the top of the sheets prior to copying, so that pupils have the targets in front of them as they work. These can be used in conjunction with the Editing checklists on pages 7–9.

On pages 10–19 there is a little booklet: 'It's Fun to Write Tip Sheets'. These can be printed and bound to make a useful reference booklet for pupils, or sheets can be given individually to pupils as and when required.

Links to the National Curriculum

The sheets in **Boost Creative Writing** will help Year 5 and 6 pupils to develop their composition skills, as set out in the National Curriculum for England (2014).

Composition

The sheets in **Boost Creative Writing** help pupils to plan their writing, by providing a structured format for discussing and recording their ideas. The sheets provide pupils with the opportunity to write for a variety of different genre and audiences. Some sample pieces of writing are given, but pupils would benefit from discussing and analysing the structure, vocabulary and grammar used in other similar texts. When writing narratives pupils are encouraged to look at the development of characters and settings.

All pupils, but especially SEN pupils, will find it very beneficial to have the opportunity to talk about what they are going to write prior to doing so, as often pupils' writing ability lags behind their speaking ability. Composing and rehearsing sentences orally, prior to writing, helps them to build a varied and rich vocabulary and encourages an increased range of sentence structures.

The sheets in this book can be used to help children to become aware of, and start to use, features of writing. In narratives, the structured format of the sheets encourages them to think and talk about the setting, characters and plot. Similarly, for non-narrative pieces, the way the sheets are formatted encourages pupils to think about how they will structure their writing.

When pupils have finished their writing, they should be encouraged to re-read their work and to think about how it can be improved. The editing checklists on pages 7–9 and the It's Fun to Write Tip Sheets on pages 10–19 will help with this. Discussing their work with you and with other pupils will help them to assess the effectiveness of their own writing.

Reading their writing aloud helps children to see that their writing is valued. Encourage pupils to use appropriate intonation and to control the tone and volume so that the meaning is clear.

Vocabulary, grammar and punctuation

Many of the sheets contain suggested vocabulary to encourage children to extend their range of vocabulary and prompt them to use new words in their writing. The activities can also be used to reinforce children's understanding of grammar and punctuation, but this is not the primary purpose of the sheets.

Suggested writing targets

To have an opening, middle and ending in my writing
To understand how to use paragraphs in my writing
To understanding the story mountain structure of narrative writing: opening, build up, climax, resolution, ending
To discuss and plan my story before writing using a story mountain or mind map
To use interesting verbs when writing the build-up part of the story
To use powerful adjectives in a description
To describe a character in detail
To describe a setting in detail
To use a range of adjectives, powerful verbs and adverbs to make the description sparkle
To understand the main ways authors use to start a story: setting, character, speech, statement or a question
To write 3 story starters using the different ways authors employ
To write an interesting opening paragraph with a hook to keep the reader interested
To check that I am writing in the same tense
To read over my writing, checking that I have put in capital letters and full stops
To use time connectives to start my sentences in different ways: Then… Suddenly… Next minute… Meanwhile… Eventually…
To use speech marks correctly and start a new line when someone is speaking
To use a repeating line in a poem
To plan and write an information booklet
To recount real events in the order they happened
To write a descriptive poem using personification or simile to paint an image in words
To use sensory description in my writing – What can you see? hear? smell? taste? How are you feeling?
To use connectives to elongate my sentences
To establish a different viewpoint in writing
To present different sides of a viewpoint
To use techniques to create suspense or excitement, such as varying sentence length or asking a question
To take time reading over my work: check for punctuation, grammar, spelling errors or omitted words needed for meaning
To create interesting opening lines to really grip the reader's interest

Editing checklist – newspaper reports

(a factual recount retelling a real event)

	✓
Interesting heading Snappy, memorable, alliterative	
Opening paragraph Answer questions Who? What? When Where? Why? Give a brief outline of the story	
Expand events in the order that they happened Use paragraphs Use time connectives: Firstly… After that… Next… Finally…	
Vivid language, powerful verbs To get an emotional reaction from the reader. 'She was *horrified* to discover…'	
Quotes eg Mrs Jones, survivor of the disaster, said " … "	
Past tense Use 'had', 'was', 'went'	
Third person Use 'he', 'she', 'they'	
Sum up eg There will be an inquiry into this catastrophe. This newspaper will keep you posted.	
Reported by (Reporter's name)	

Editing checklist – narrative writing

	✓
Clear structure of plot Introduction, middle, ending Story mountain structure	
Paragraphs 4+	
Interesting vocabulary Replace over-used words	
Build up description – adjectives Imagery: simile, metaphor, personification. What do you see? hear? smell? taste? feel?	
Create suspense Paragraph hook	
Vary sentence length Short sentences for suspense and action. Longer sentences for description.	
Use connectives Next… After a while… Meanwhile… etc	
Reader understanding Have you written what you meant to say?	
Speech New line for each new speaker	
Tense – past or present? Keep in the same tense	
Written in 1st (I) or 3rd person (name)	
Edit and shave Cut out unnecessary details	
Punctuation check	
Spelling and grammar check	

Editing checklist – persuasive writing

(an argument from a particular point of view: poster, leaflet, advert, letter, article)

	✓
Catchy or alliterative phrase On advert, leaflet or poster	
Clear information Decide on your viewpoint and organize the information to support it	
Ask a question Do you want to…? Would you like it if…? Can you really…?	
Powerful language It is important to… You must realize…	
Simple psychology Everybody knows… You would be foolish not to…	
Present tense Use verbs 'is', 'are', 'have', 'can', 'like to', 'should be'	
Facts to support your point of view	
Connectives As a result of… Therefore… Consequently… etc	
Closing statement to reinforce/repeat viewpoint All the evidence shows… It's quite clear that…	
Illustration On advert, leaflet or poster	

Editing checklist – instructional writing

(an explanatory account: recipes, rules, 'how to make…', 'how to play…' etc)

	✓
List of ingredients/equipment needed	
Ordered step-by-step approach	
Bullet points or numbers for each step	
Clear, short, simple sentences	
Imperative (or bossy) verbs to start each instruction Use present tense: Heat… Mix… Stir… etc	
Time connectives to start each instruction First… Then… Next… After that…	
Final point eg Eat and enjoy!	
Illustration(s)?	

Editing checklist – discursive writing

(an account giving different sides of a viewpoint)

	✓	
Introductory statement about the topic you are discussing		
Arguments for And reasons		
Arguments against And reasons		
Paragraphs for each viewpoint		
Quotes as evidence eg: I spoke to Mr Smith, the Head Teacher, and he told me that...'		
Powerful connectives Obviously... Nevertheless... Therefore...		
Summary Sum up the discussion and give your point of view		

Editing checklist – non-chronological report writing

(a factual recount written in any order – after the introduction – about an animal, country, person or historical event)

	✓	
Information Gathered mainly from books or the Internet		
Planned and clearly organized		
General introduction and opening statement		
Headings and paragraphs		
Present tense Use verbs 'is', 'are', 'have', 'can', 'like to', 'should be'		
Factual sentences		
Technical vocabulary To do with the subject matter		
Precise descriptive vocabulary eg Hamsters are inquisitive active pets.		
Pictures/fun features eg dog facts written in a paw		

It's Fun to Write

Contents

	page
Do's and don'ts for planning	3
Planning and organizing story writing	4
Build up description: characters	5
Build up description: setting	7–9
Use imagery	10
Involve the senses	11–12
Create suspense or excitement	13–14
Replace over-used words with powerful verbs	15–16
Different ways to start sentences: use connectives	17
Check punctuation	18
Story writing tips	19

Tip Sheets

Do's and don'ts for planning

Don't rush into writing!

Do spend up to 10 minutes brainstorming and planning ideas.

Don't worry about writing sentences when brainstorming ideas.

Do use key words and phrases to remind you of your ideas.

Do make sure your ideas relate to the story topic.

Don't forget to arrange your ideas in logical order.

Do aim for a minimum of four paragraphs.

Do have an introduction, middle section and an ending

Planning and organizing story writing

Introduction
Set the scene and mood. Make it interesting so the reader wants to read on. There are five main ways to start a story:
- Description of character
- Description of setting
- A question
- Speech
- A statement

Middle section
Use the story mountain format in narrative story writing. Have a sequence of events. What happens next? Then? After that?

Build up: climb up the mountain, set the scene, something starts to happen.

Climax: reach the top or high point in your story when something exciting happens.

Resolution: climb down the mountain. What are the results of the climax?

Ending
Tie up any loose ends. It is lazy to end a story by saying 'it was all a dream'. Try using a sentence which links back to the title – a surprise or shock ending – involving the reader by saying what the character has learnt.

Build up description: characters

Build	average height, chubby, lean, muscular, plump, short, slender, slim, skinny, tall
Hair	bleached blonde, dark brown, golden brown, fair haired, ginger, red, jet black, snow white, silvery grey dishevelled, frizzy, greasy, matted, tangled, thick, thinning, uncombed glossy, shiny, neatly combed bald, curly, long, pigtails, ponytail, plaits, short, wavy
Skin	clammy, freckled, lily white, lined, pale, pasty-looking, pimpled, pockmarked, scarred, suntanned, spotty, weather-beaten, wrinkled
Eyes	beady, dark brown, deep set, emerald green, sky blue, stone grey
Teeth	crooked, decaying, pearly white, protruding, razor like, rotten, sharp, yellow
Other features	birthmark, bushy eyebrows, hairy wart, long straggly beard, mole, unshaven, whiskers on chin
Hands	beautifully manicured, bitten nails, claw-like fingers, curved nails, purple veined
Voice	husky, like a foghorn, softly spoken, stuttering, wheezy, whining
Personality	(Don't forget to imply through actions) anxious, bad-tempered, boastful, cruel, cunning, finicky, foolish, fussy, greedy, grumpy, impish, irritable, lazy, long-suffering, malicious, mean, mischievous, nasty, powerful, proud, revolting, selfish, scatter-brained, silly, spiteful, vain brave, cheerful, clever, courageous, curious, eager, enthusiastic, friendly, heroic, intelligent, jolly, happy, optimistic, hard-working, warm-hearted, wise

Expression and look	blank stare, dreamy look, glaring with anger, shame-faced, sullen, unblinking attractive, beautiful, fearsome, loathsome, repulsive, revolting, ugly
Walk	strode determinedly, sauntered cheerfully, limped painfully, marched crossly
Use adverbs to describe how the character does something	angrily, anxiously, apprehensively, bravely, calmly, carefully, carelessly, cautiously, cheerfully, clumsily, crossly, eagerly, easily, earnestly, excitedly, fearfully, furiously, gently, gladly, gratefully, greedily, grumpily, happily, hopefully, hungrily, hurriedly, impatiently, lazily, magically, mysteriously, nastily, nervously, noisily, obediently, patiently, politely, proudly, quietly, quickly, rapidly, rudely, roughly, sadly, selfishly, silently, sleepily, slowly, softly, swiftly, tearfully, thoughtfully, violently, willingly

Build up description: setting

Time of day	Light conditions
dawn	hazy rosy glow as dawn broke
early morning	sunshine streamed through the windows
lunchtime	searing blinding light
mid afternoon	dull dismal day
dusk	dimly lit... brightly lit
twilight	lengthening shadows
evening	pitch black
late evening	moonlight filtered through
midnight	stars glistened like diamonds in the moonlit sky

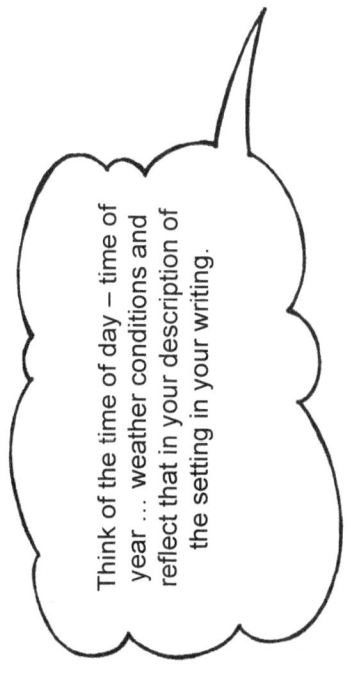

Think of the time of day – time of year ... weather conditions and reflect that in your description of the setting in your writing.

Weather

hot, cold, rainy, snowy, spring-like summery, autumnal, wintry	drizzling rain	chilly
	rain drummed rhythmically down	shrouded in damp mist
	sodden grass	autumnal leaves rustled underfoot
	dewdrops glistened in spiders' webs	dry withered leaves
	hot sunny weather	lightning zigzagged across the sky
	scented roses were entwined up the wall	torrential downpour
	water from a fountain trickled into a pool	howling wind
	waves splashed on to the warm sand	leaden grey sky
	puffy clouds	stillness ... powdery snow
	azure blue sky	frosty ground
	cloudless	white blanket of snow
	sun drenched	icicle gleamed like a glass dagger
	scorching...sweltering	bare leafless trees
	hot ... muggy	blades of grass were stiff with frost
	airless	bleak sunless landscape
	crystal clear	bitterly cold
	tranquil	wind swept
	warm starlit night	biting easterly wind

Use imagery

Use a simile
❖ Compare one thing with another, using the words 'like' and 'as'.

The leaves spun wildly on the tree like shiny discs.
The sun was like a round mirror gleaming in the sky.

Use a metaphor
❖ Describe something as if it was something else.

The mother duck was a lioness defending her chicks.
The balls of cotton wool glided across the sky.

Use personification
❖ Give a human quality to something that is not human.

Ivy twisted its fingers around the bark of the tree.
The floorboards groaned under the weight of the heavy suitcase.

Use alliteration
❖ Repeat particular sound in a series of words.

Waves of warm air wafted across my face.
The spotted snake slid slowly down the path.

> Use similes, metaphors, personification, alliteration sparingly to develop description, and maximize the dramatic effect.

Build up description: setting

Short phrases to describe an old attic room

👂	...ancient floorboard creaked ...the rusty door hinge squeaked open ...rain drummed rhythmically on the roof
👁	The antique oak door at the top of the staircase had a burnished brass knob which gleamed in the dim light. Shafts of moonlight filtered through a small window in the rafter. ...a sliver of light came from behind the closed door ...the flashlight flickered and a shadowy shape danced across the wall ...old trunks full of long forgotten toys ...spotted a small black chest, slightly worse for wear, covered in a layer of dust
👃	...a musty smell of damp and mildew ...smelt an aroma of musky mothballs
✋	...felt a cold blast of air sweep over me ...a silky cobweb brushed against my face
💭	Was it my imagination, or was something moving over there? The diary had been hidden away for all those years, and I was delighted to have found it.

> Involve the senses to make the reader feel part of your story and create an atmosphere. What can you see? hear? feel? smell? touch? taste?

> Choose adjectives, adverbs and powerful verbs and some sensory description in your portrayal of the setting.

Involve the senses

Hear		See	
banged	murmured	attractive	glittering
bawled	popped	beautiful	gloomy
boomed	rattled	bleached	glowing
bubbled	roared	blemished	grimy
buzzed	rumbled	blurred	indistinct
cackled	rustled	bulky	marbled
chimed	scraped	burnished	mottled
chirped	screeched	carved	murky
chuckled	shattered	clean	patterned
clattered	shuffled	cluttered	polished
clicked	sizzled	crinkled	pointed
clinked	slammed	crumpled	reflective
crackled	snapped	dark	rusty
creaked	snarled	dazzling	shadowy
crunched	snored	dim	shimmering
droned	splashed	dingy	shiny
drummed	spluttered	dirty	smeared
echoed	squeaked	discoloured	smudged
fizzed	squealed	dull	sparkling
grated	squelched	faded	speckled
groaned	swished	flecked	spiralled
growled	tinkled	freckled	spotted
gurgled	twittered	fuzzy	stained
hissed	wailed	gaudy	striped
howled	whimpered	glossy	streaked
hummed	whirred	gorgeous	tarnished
jingled	whispered	gleaming	thick
lapped	whistled	glimmering	transparent
moaned	zoomed	glistening	twinkling

Feel	Smell	Touch	Taste
alarmed	aroma	bony	acidic
appreciative	aromatic	bristly	bitter
bewildered	decayed	bumpy	burnt
cheerful	festering	clammy	butterscotch
confused	fishy	cold	chocolate
excited	foul	crispy	creamy
delighted	fragrance	dry	delicious
dejected	fragranced	fluffy	insipid
embarrassed	fragrant	furry	juicy
furious	fresh	greasy	lemon
guilty	fusty	gritty	luscious
happy	musty	hairy	mouth watering
impatient	mouldy	oily	scrumptious
lonely	mildewed	prickly	sickly
nervous	odour	ridged	sour
offended	perfumed	rough	spicy
overjoyed	pungent	scaly	stale
overwhelmed	putrid	scratchy	strawberry
pleased	rank	silky	sugary
sad	reeking	slimy	sweet
satisfied	rotten	slippery	syrupy
shocked	scent	smooth	tangy
subdued	scented	spiky	tart
tearful	smell	soft	tasty
troubled	smelly	sticky	tasteless
uncertain	spicy	stubby	vanilla
uncomfortable	stale	velvety	vinegary
upset	stench	wet	watery
worried	whiff	warm	zesty

Create suspense or excitement

Use some short sentences

- I sat bolt upright in bed. The sound of shattering glass had woken me up.
- Horror struck, I froze to the spot.
- A cold shiver went down my spine.
- The fox slunk silently into the yard. He sniffed the night air. Then he crept towards the henhouse.

Ask questions

- She could not believe it was for her. What was in the box?
- Unnerved, Molly began to walk quicker. Were those footsteps behind her?
- Was it my imagination or did something move in the corner of the room?

Tease and keep the reader guessing

Build up the sense of expectancy by hinting rather than telling the reader straightaway what your character is going to do or the event or danger that is about to happen.

For example, on a journey to pick up a much wanted animal from the pet shop, keep hinting about the excitement to come by concentrating on the details of the car journey, the inside of the shop etc before revealing the purpose of the outing.

Use vocabulary to build up scary tension

creepy	deserted	draped in cobwebs
echoing	eerie	chilling
pale ghostly moon	pitch black	menacing
mysterious	neglected	streak of lightning
shrouded in mist	shadowy shape	sinister
spooky atmosphere	high pitched sound reverberated	the church clock chimed midnight

Use a hook at the end of a paragraph

- The noise of the doorbell echoed through the house. Holly rushed to open the door but there was no one there. She looked to the left and to the right but the street was empty; no one was astir. Then she saw the box which had been left by the front door.

Make the mood and pace of the story vary. Have a balance of suspense, with short snappy sentences mixed with a more relaxed descriptive tone. This will serve to increase interest and heighten tension.

Remember short sentences build up suspense and longer sentences build up description.

Replace overused words with powerful verbs

said

asked	gasped	promised	stated
argued	giggled	pronounced	sniggered
bawled	groaned	questioned	taunted
begged	grumbled	remarked	teased
cackled	insisted	replied	whined
chuckled	interrupted	screamed	whispered
complained	inquired	screeched	yelled
cried	joked	scolded	wept
declared	mumbled	shouted	
demanded	murmured	sighed	
exclaimed	pleaded	sobbed	

went

ambled	hurtled	scudded	strolled
climbed	inched	scurried	tiptoed
crawled	jumped	scuttled	trudged
crept	limped	shuffled	tumbled
dashed	marched	skedaddled	wafted
drifted	plunged	slithered	walked
floated	ran	soared	wandered
flew	raced	sped	wriggled
hopped	rushed	sprinted	zoomed
hovered	sauntered	staggered	
hurried	scampered	stomped	

shone

beamed	flickered	glistened	shimmered
blazed	gleamed	glittered	smouldered
burned	glimmered	glowed	sparkled
flashed	glinted	radiated	twinkled

saw

beheld	glimpsed	perceived	spotted
detected	identified	recognized	unearthed
discovered	noticed	set eyes on	witnessed
distinguished	observed	spied	

frightened

alarmed	intimidated	scared	unnerved
appalled	panicked	startled	upset
horrified	petrified	terrified	worried

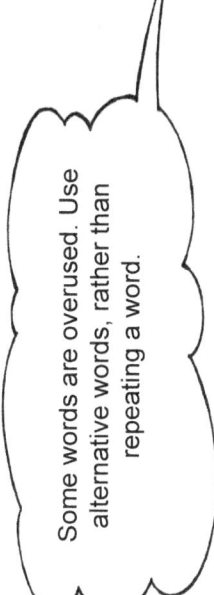

Some words are overused. Use alternative words, rather than repeating a word.

Check punctuation

Capital letters
- Beginning of a sentence
- Name of a person or place
- Days of the week
- Months of the year

Commas
- Lists
  We went to the shops to get butter, sugar and eggs for the pie.
- After speech
  "I can come to the party," said Tom.
- To make sentences clear
  As a matter of fact, I'd love to.

Exclamation marks
- If something is felt strongly
  Help, I'm stuck!

Question marks
- To ask questions
  What is your name?

Apostrophes
- To make words smaller
  <u>I am</u>   –   <u>I'm</u> coming to see you.

Speech marks
- When someone is talking
  "Who is it?" whispered Amber

Different ways to start sentences: use connectives

One day…	Once upon a time…
A long time ago…	During the holidays…
A few months ago…	When I woke up…
Initially…	From the word go…
Just then…	At that precise moment…
Suddenly…	All of a sudden…
At once…	Immediately…
Quick as a flash…	Instantly…
In no time at all…	In the nick of time…
Unexpectedly…	Without warning…
Surprisingly…	Out of the blue…
Meanwhile…	On the other hand…
A split second later…	A moment later…
Next minute…	Before he knew it…
A little while later…	Before long…
Shortly afterwards…	As an afterthought…
After some time…	Later that day…
Eventually…	At the last minute…
Finally…	In conclusion…
When it was all over…	The following week…

Story writing tips

1. **Organize and plan your story**
   - Allow up to 10 minutes planning time.
   - Write in first person (I) or third person (he/she/it).
   - Make sure your writing relates to the topic throughout. Don't lose focus!

2. **Remember paragraphs**
   - Indent each pararaph or leave a line between each.
   - Paragraphs usually have 4–7 sentences.
   - Paragraphs usually have one main idea.
   - End each paragraph with a gripping sentence, as a hook.

3. **Build up description of character and setting using interesting vocabulary**
   - Paint a picture with words to help the reader imagine a scene.
   - Think of interesting vocabulary and powerful verbs.
   - Use adjectives to make your writing more descriptive.
   - Try to use similes and metaphors to make descriptions vivid.
   - Use senses. What can you see? hear? smell? taste? How are you feeling?

4. **Create suspense and vary sentence length to maintain reader interest**
   - Use long sentences for description.
   - Use short sentences to give an impression of suspense, action or speed.

5. **Keep in the same tense**
   - It is easier to write in the past tense than the present tense.

6. **Use connectives**
   - Start your sentences in different ways to make your writing flow. Use, for example:
   Then... Suddenly... Next minute... Meanwhile... Eventually..., etc

7. **Replace overused words if you need to mention something twice**
   - For example:
   saw – glimpsed, spied, noticed, etc

8. **Use direct speech sparingly**
   - It can become long and boring and be difficult to punctuate.
   - Start a new line when someone is speaking.

9. **Take time to read over what you have written**
   - Check your punctuation, spelling and grammar.
   - Check to see if you have left out words needed for meaning.

10. **Edit and shave**
    - Cut out unnecessary details which don't add interest or are not needed to give meaning to the story.

Amusing animal adventure story

Title: _____

Who?
Weave the description of the animal into your story.

Ideas:
Appearance: size? look/feel of skin or fur? Special features? Walk?
Personality: timid, daring, cheeky, good natured, kindly, greedy

Setting
What does the animal see, hear, smell and feel? Use senses and simile to heighten the description. Add detail, so the readers feel they are there.

Ideas: dog in a pet shop...   horse in a stable...   mouse in hole in farmhouse...

Character
Add detail!

Ideas:
Shy dog was worried about going to a new home and having a new owner
Fat, out of condition horse wanted to lose weight and win a race
Bold mouse enjoyed going into the farmhouse and finding cheese

What happens next? Then what? After that?

Ideas:
Dog loved new home, made a friend, found something valuable when looking for bones. Who? What?
Horse found another animal to act as his personal trainer and who helped him get fit. Who? How?
Mouse got caught in a mousetrap before he could reach safety. How? Who saved him?

How is the animal feeling at the end of the story?

The secret in the attic

 Adventure story

Title: _____

Main character?

Setting
What time of day: early morning? evening? Reflect that atmosphere in your story.

Describe step-by-step the journey up to the attic: staircase, attic door, handle. What could you hear? see? smell? Use similes or personification. How were you feeling?

Ideas:　　floorboards creaked　　　well-worn steps… ivory handle shaped like…polished oak door

　strong smell of spicy cinnamon wafted　　　apprehensive… curious… excited…

Describe the room
Ideas: dimly lit… dusty… shaft of light flickered through… beamed roof…

What did you find?
Ideas: old diary… egg… antique pocket watch…

What is special about your find?

Ideas:
Diary belonged to a distant relative
Something unusual hatched from the egg
Watch enabled you to go back or forward in time.

What happened next? Then what? After that?

What were your thoughts about the find?

The unwelcome animal visitor in the night

Write from the point of view of a hen or mouse.

Title: _____

Set the scene
Describe the night. What can be seen? heard?
Use similes and personification to heighten description.

Ideas: distant hoot of owl... pale ghostly moon... silhouetted... shadowy shape...

In the hen house/mouse hole
Portray a cosy environment. Give the hen or mouse human characteristics.
Is there someone in the family who is a bit slow to get ready for bed, or another who is fussy, etc.

Outside the hen house/mouse hole
Add detail.
Something is moving. Contrast how the peaceful mood changes as anxiety sets in with the arrival of the unwelcome visitor – use your senses.

What could be seen of the visitor from the hen house or mouse hole?

What or who saved the hens/mice from attack?
What happened next? Then what happened? Describe in detail.

What happened to the unwelcome visitor?
Was he hurt?

What are the thoughts of the hen or mouse when the danger has passed?

This page may be photocopied for use by the purchasing institution only.

Boost Creative Writing, Years 5–6
© Judith Thornby and Brilliant Publications Limited

Adventure story

The unwelcome animal visitor in the night

Write, draw and label a mind map of ideas. Be descriptive!

What could be seen?
colours/texture/size
cluttered… tidy… squashed… roomy…

What could be heard?

What is the character feeling?

What could be smelt?

Movement/actions
powerful verbs

Boost Creative Writing, Years 5–6
© Judith Thornby and Brilliant Publications Limited

Adventure story

A spooky tale

Write a descriptive story about a man who sheltered from a storm in an old run-down house in the woods.

Title: _____

Setting – build the atmosphere
Describe the stormy weather.
Is it spring, summer, autumn or winter? Reflect the season in your description.
Use similes and personification to build up the description.
Vocabulary: lightning zigzagged across the sky.

Describe the house
Add detail.
Describe the overgrown garden, full of brambles, and the run-down house.
Bring in the senses: What could the man see? hear? smell? What was he thinking?

Ideas: derelict house… ivy twined up the walls like… broken, cracked roof tiles… dark and dingy smell… cobwebs draped…

Describe certain obstacles that the man had to deal with
Ideas: locked door … how did he get into the house?
Slippery, threadbare carpet… Did he nearly have an accident?
Sense that some ghostly presence was watching him… Why?
Loose floorboard creaked… How did he feel?

What did he find inside the house?
Ideas: old diary… scrapbook…

What were the man's thoughts when the storm was over and he could leave? Did the experience affect him?

The strange encounter in the school library

Title: _____

It was the end of a busy day and all was quiet in the school. Or was it? What was happening in the school library?

Who?
Why did he/she go into the library after school? Homework task? Odd noise?
Build up the atmosphere. What was seen? heard? smelt? felt?
Use similes and personification in your descriptions.

What happened next? Add detail!
Ideas:
Open a book and pictures start to move … What book? What pictures moved?
A character from a book is in the library… Who? Why do you recognize the character?
A door appears in the wall and…

Then what happened? After that? Then? Meanwhile?

Ideas:
Character from book wants you to follow them…
You are actually in part of the story…

How did it end?
Ideas: the sound of the school bell in the distance breaks spell…
What happened to the story book character?

How did it affect the person?

Adventure story

The strange encounter in the school library

Read this story beginning:

> Reading isn't my strong point and I am not very keen on it. I don't find it very entertaining. In fact I think it is a waste of time. So I was not best pleased when my English teacher, Miss Penwell, told us we had to write about our favourite book as a homework task. Furthermore she expected the work to be handed in by the next day.
>
> Anyway I had a spare half hour after school, so I reluctantly decided to go to the library. There was nobody but me in the room. I was browsing through the books, idly flicking through the pages when I spotted a rather large book, at least 60 centimetres wide, hidden on a bottom shelf. It was bound in dark green leather and covered in cobwebs. There was a sickly sweet smell coming from it, like sticky toffee boiling in a pan. Of course I had to have a proper look at the book...

Discuss this writing

◆ How has the writer started the story?
   ❖ Character description
   ❖ Setting description
   ❖ Speech
   ❖ Question
   ❖ Statement

◆ How has the writer made the reader feel part of the story?

◆ Can you comment on the language used?

A scary story

Opening

I was lost and alone in a solitary wasteland and night was falling like a dark blanket. It was then that I heard a low menacing howl quite nearby. I looked around and glimpsed the orange eyes of a lone wolf gleaming fiercely in the dim light. It was hungry and had caught my scent.

Without a moment's delay, I took to my heels and raced frantically towards a small coppice of trees for shelter. I knew I was in great danger as the wolf gave chase. Then I spotted the huge mansion which was half hidden in the wood, its tall towers loomed up into the dark sky. With all my energy I willed my legs to run faster and faster until I finally reached it. I pounded desperately on the door and it opened immediately, so I tore inside banging the door shut behind me.

Middle part – Who is behind the door?
Continue the story in the same style, focusing on the senses to build up descriptive tension. (Use the second sheet to help you.)

Ending

A little while later, I tumbled into the bed provided for me. All the anxiety had worn me out and I fell straight asleep. Suddenly...

Build up tension, but give a twist to the story by implying something dreadful is going to happen, when really it doesn't.

A scary story

Write the middle of the story in the same style as the opening, creating some tension.

Who is behind the door? Set the scene: How do you feel? What can you hear in the room?

Ideas:

Feelings	
scared frightened (how can you imply this?)	hands shook… heart beat widely…
Noises	
door	creaked
log fire	crackled
clock	chimed
wind	rattled
footsteps	shuffled
Who do you see? (mysterious gentleman… manservant…) What does the person look like?	
height	tall figure
walk	strode… limped…
eyes	deep set bright beady
expression/look	unblinking blank stare
skin	freckled, lily white, pale, pimpled, wrinkled, pockmarked face
hair/facial hair	ginger, jet black, snow white, silvery, greasy, matted, thinning, long haired, bushy eyebrows, straggly beard
voice (speech)	"I've been expecting you," murmured a man in a voice booming like a foghorn.

Choose any words in the grid that fit in with the character you have thought of. Add your own words, using a thesaurus if needed.

The bubble that manages to break free and escape

Title: _____

"It's so lovely to be free," the bubble thought with relief.

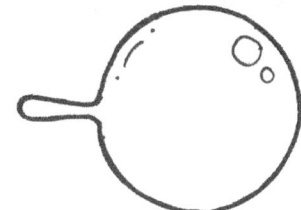

Where?
Use simile and personification in your description. What does the bubble look like? How is the bubble feeling?

Ideas: water bubble in a saucepan… air bubble in lemonade… soap bubble in bath…

Vocabulary: hot, cramped, claustrophobic, depressed, sad, restless, agitated, keyed up, translucent, lustrous, opaque, luminous, etc.

What happened next? How did it break free?
Ideas:
Grew bigger?
Thicker?
Stronger?
Changed colour?
Thought powerful thoughts?

Then what happened? After that? Then? Meanwhile?

Ideas: into the garden… high up into the sky… over the sea… to a different country…

Vocabulary: floated, skimmed across, gradually gained momentum

What happened next? After that? Then?
What did the bubble see? hear? smell? touch?
How was it feeling as it went on its journey?

Did it end happily for the bubble or not?

First person fantasy story

What happened when you bought an unusual present from a shop?

Title: _____

Interesting starting sentence

Where was the shop? How did it look from the outside?
Did you find the shop by accident? Were you looking for it?
Make the reader feel involved. Describe the setting in detail.

Ideas: down a deserted side street… on the outskirts of town… in a busy airport…

What sort of shop was it inside? Add detail!
Ideas: antique shop… toy shop… sports shop… gift shop…

What things caught your eye? What did you buy?
Anything unusual about it – strangely light/heavy… odd colour, etc.

What about the sales assistant?
Did he/she remind you of anyone? – Merlin-type or fairy godmother type character, etc.
Did he/she warn you about your purchase?

What happened next? Was it a present for you or for someone else?

What happened next that caused a bit of trouble?
Ideas: during the day… the following day…

Was the trouble resolved? What were your feelings about it all?

A descriptive account of a beach

Heighten your description with the use of similes, metaphors and personification. Bring in the senses and use interesting verbs.

Title: _____

What can you see?

Ideas: sun, sand, sea, waves, clouds, palm trees, rock pools, cliffs, boats, fish, crabs, shells, seaweed, coral, rocks, lighthouse, grassy dunes, lights

What can you hear?

Ideas: children, waves, seagulls, surf, wind

What can you smell?

Ideas: salty spray, ozone, sun tan oil, decaying seaweed

What can you taste?

Ideas: perspiration, food from vendor?

How do you feel?

Ideas: relaxed, happy, soothed, calm, refreshed, peaceful

A descriptive account of a beach

Read this descriptive account:

> It was quieter on the beach now and the light had dimmed as the sun slowly set. The evening breeze tickled my skin and ruffled my long hair playfully as I sat on the cold stone wall. The palm trees behind me stood still and watchful.
>
> I listened to the rhythmic lapping of the waves as the water ebbed and flowed over the soft damp sand. The sea seemed more at peace now compared to the angry heave and swell of surf earlier in the day.
>
> I watched the solid shape of a huge liner etched against the horizon move steadily onwards. I stayed put for a short while until the moon gently painted the water with silvery light, and the stars, like tiny diamonds, started to twinkle in the night sky.
>
> I was roused from my reverie by the delicious aroma of tapas coming from a familiar restaurant on the other side of the road. I inhaled the salty tang of the sea and breathed a silent sigh of contentment as I made my way quickly to my workplace again. I felt refreshed and invigorated by the brief period of time that I had spent on the beach.

Discuss this writing

- What time of day is it? How do you know?
- How has the writer made the reader involved?
- What descriptive devices have been used?

A day in your life which you remember well

Title: _____

Interesting starting sentence

Idea: I remember the day clearly because of what happened. It all started…

Build up the atmosphere of excitement
Don't give too much away at this stage. Make the reader feel involved. What do you remember seeing? hearing? tasting? smelling? How were you feeling?

When?
Ideas: a school day… weekday… weekend…

Where are you at first?
Ideas: at home getting ready to… at the hospital waiting… in a car going to…

What was about to happen that would made the day memorable?

Ideas:
starting a new school
moving into a new house
having a special birthday treat

seeing a baby brother or sister for the first time
collecting a new puppy, kitten or other pet

What happened at first?
Describe in detail, step-by-step.

Then what happened? After that?

What are your feelings now about that day?

Boost Creative Writing, Years 5–6
© Judith Thornby and Brilliant Publications Limited

Rescue from the Titanic

Set the scene
Who? (man/woman/child/rich/poor)

Where were you on the boat on the night the Titanic hit the iceberg?

What did you do when you realized the Titanic was sinking?
Describe order of events in the right order, step-by-step.
How did you get to the top deck?
Did you get into a lifeboat?
What could you see? hear? smell? How were you feeling?

How did you escape? What are your lasting memories?

Vocabulary

shuddered	rammed	iceberg	top deck
jostled	fight for survival	eerie	perpendicular
musicians played on	terrified	bitterly cold	fingers numb
swamped by waves	horror	darkest hour before dawn	

Read quotes from survivors and weave them into your story.

Rescue from the Titanic

Beginning
Who? Where were you on the boat?
Opening lines need to interest the reader.

Middle
What did you do when you realized the Titanic was sinking?
Remember the different senses: sounds, sights, smells, tastes, touch.
What were you feeling? Use dramatic words: imagery, simile, metaphor.

Conclusion
How did you escape? What are your lasting memories?

Dear Diary

What did Theseus write in his diary the day he killed the Minotaur?

Opening sentence

Dear Diary,
You won't believe the day I've had today…

What was it like in the labyrinth?

What could you hear?   What could you see?

What could you smell?    How were you feeling

What was the Minotaur like? How did you kill it?
What did the Minotaur look like? What did he smell like? How were you feeling?

Vocabulary:
half man half bull	hideous	strong	frightful red eyes
glared	bellowed	worried	fierce battle
Instantly…	After a while…	Quick as a flash…	Finally…

How did you find your way out of the labyrinth?
Are you glad? Why?

Vocabulary: magic thread… Ariadne, daughter of King Minos

Closing sentence
Idea: Anyway, I can't wait to tell father I've killed the Minotaur…

My newspaper report

Pick a well-known story and write your version as a newspaper report. Give your version a twist!

Headline
(Make it catchy)

Write down your facts in the correct order
Pick one story. Answer the questions:

When?

Who?

Where was the person?

What was the person doing?

Why was he/she doing it?

What happened?

Questions for reporter to ask?

Idea (to ask the wolf in The Three Little Pigs): Why did you blow the pigs' house down?

Add quotes
(What people involved in the story said)

Ideas:
"I am disgusted that the children…" the witch told me.
"Humpty knows that he should not…" said his mother.

My newspaper report

Reporter:

A day in the sweatshop – plan for report

What are sweatshops?
Sweatshops, or sweat factories as they are sometimes called, are places where people are employed to make goods cheaply and where they are treated badly.

Pay
poorly paid
children expected
 to do adult jobs
less than minimum
 wage

Sweatshops

Working hours/hazards
long 12-hour day
tiredness causing accidents
few breaks
fingers trapped in machines
no proper training
hardly any days off

Types of jobs
using sewing machines
stitching
mixing chemicals

Factory conditions
filthy… cramped
lots of people sleeping in
 factory
unhygienic
eyes irritated by chemicals
 in dyes and fibres
little proper nourishment

Write a diary entry about a day working in a sweatshop.
Use and expand the ideas in the plan.

A day in the sweatshop – a diary entry

Tuesday evening

I woke up this morning and just could not face another hard day's work at the factory. I know that I have to do the work because it is so difficult to get a job and somebody else will just take my place...

What snacks should be allowed in school?

Should the only snacks allowed at school be fruit? Discuss and give your point of view.

Introduce argument

Ideas: There is an argument for and against promoting fruit and banning sweets, cakes and chocolate as snacks in school.

Reasons for? Add detail

Ideas:
Increase brain power
More tasty
Feel good factor

Full of glucose which gives energy
Look forward to…

Reasons against? Add detail

Ideas:
Unhealthy/better for you
Cause allergic reaction
Causes litter

Rot your teeth
Could spoil appetite

Quote(s) supporting the case for or against

Idea: *I spoke to _____ who told me…*

Head teacher   Pupil   Caretaker   Canteen manager

Sum up and give your point of view

Ideas:
Obviously…
Nevertheless…
Therefore…

Persuasive article for the Nursery Rhyme Gazette

Title:
Should _____

Reported by: _____

Opening
The *Nursery Rhyme Gazette* newspaper carefully presents both sides of an argument. This week we are discussing whether:

Ideas:
Should Wolf be blamed for scaring Little Red Riding Hood?
Should Goldilocks be charged for breaking into the Bear family home?
Should Mrs Dumpty be blamed for being a poor mother?

Reasons for? Add detail	**Reasons against? Add detail**

Quote(s) supporting the case for or against

Ideas:
I spoke to…
He/she said…

Sum up and give your point of view
Having given this matter with some thought…

Useful words for discussion

First of all	On the other hand	Some people would consider
It could be argued that	Many people believe	Those who think this argue
Furthermore they suggest	In addition they think	Some would argue
Finally they think	Furthermore	Obviously
In conclusion	Nevertheless	This newspaper believes
In my opinion	Therefore	Consequently

This page may be photocopied for use by the purchasing institution only.

Write and design a persuasive poster

Be an eco-friendly school!

Slogan

Layout
Plan to use all the sheet!

Illustration
Size? Detail? Colour? Position?

Facts
Make points clear.

Persuasive language

Ideas:
It is important to…
Why not…
Help by…
Think about?

Vocabulary

energy	waste	recycle	bins	paper use
double sided	switch off	stand by	close	use less
water	water butts	nature garden	pond wildlife	vegetables
compost	wormery	travel	walk	cycle
share a car	little	responsibility	improve environment	

Boost Creative Writing, Years 5–6
© Judith Thornby and Brilliant Publications Limited

This page may be photocopied for use by the purchasing institution only.

A mystery story – whodunnit?

The mystery
Ideas:

The mystery of the stolen cupcakes	The mystery of the missing blue paint	The mystery of the missing white furry kittens

The setting
Describe in detail what can be seen, heard or smelt.
Ideas:

Cook's kitchen: ... busily mixing... delicious aroma of... smell wafted out of the window... at last ready to decorate...	School caretaker's storeroom: shelves full of... everything tidily stacked away, Mr .... fussily sorting out...	Cat breeder's house: strong whiff of fish, red carpet covered in silky white cat hairs, busy vacuuming... did not hear the front door open and someone creep in...

The characters

Ideas:
Detective   Cook/caretaker/cat breeder   Suspect   Red herring

Special characteristics
Ideas:
scratches ear to think   drives a red sports car
eats a lot of sweets   very short sighted, wore thick rimmed spectacles
extra large feet   bright red hair
nervous twitch... worried expression... guilty look

The clues

Ideas:
cake crumbs leading to...   big footprints belonging to a large man in the soil
blue paint on finger   red hair left at scene
sweet wrapper left at crime scene white kitten fluff on suspect's jumper
Mr/Mrs .... was seen leaving the scene of the crime

Whodunnit? The motive
Ideas:

Wanted to win the cake competition and was jealous of the beautiful cakes made by...	Took the paint because he/she had no money to finish off painting...	Wanted to make snow shoes out of kittens' fur because he/she was an evil person

This page may be photocopied for use by the purchasing institution only.

Boost Creative Writing, Years 5–6
© Judith Thornby and Brilliant Publications Limited

Whodunnit – structure

Setting of the mystery	Set the scene. Make the reader feel as if he/she was there. What could be seen? heard? smelt?		
Introduce characters	Main character(s)	Suspect	Red herring
	Write a paragraph about each character. Add detail so the reader gets a good picture of what they look like and how they behave. What was each character thinking? Suggest that they might be the culprit and have taken something, even if they have not.		
The discovery	Something has gone missing. When or how was it discovered that something had disappeared?		
The detective is on the trail	**Either** Be the detective and work out who was the culprit, weaving it into the story. What clues led you to solve the mystery? What put you off the trail? What was the reason why it happened? What were your thoughts about it? **Or** Fill in a detective report. Who were the suspects? What were the clues? Who was the culprit? What was the motive?		
Clues			
Whodunnit?			
Motive			
Final thoughts			

Whodunnit – report by detective

What was the mystery?

Where did it take place?

Evidence/clues	Left by

Whodunnit?	Reason why?

Whodunnits – vocabulary used

detective	investigator or person who tries to solve a mystery
sidekick	assistant, helper
culprit	person who has committed a wrong doing
suspect	person detective thinks might have done something wrong
red herring	something or someone that puts detective off the trail
evidence	anything that proves someone has committed a crime
clues	signs of evidence
witness	an onlooker, observer
alibi	a good reason why a person could not have done something wrong
innocent	harmless, not guilty
guilty	has done something wrong, broken the law
motive	the reason why
interview	ask someone questions to find out what they think or know
confess	own up, come clean

The case of the missing prize pumpkin

It all started one chilly day last September. The famous detective Sam Gumshoe was relaxing in his penthouse flat in Baker Street stroking his dog Basil, a rather clever West Highland Terrier, when the phone rang. It was a Mr Trowel who was a member of the local gardening group in Gerrards Cross. He sounded almost tearful and wanted Sam Gumshoe's urgent help.

Having nothing better to do, Sam decided to pay Mr Trowel a visit. Donning his blue checked blazer which he always wore, whether the weather was hot or cold, he whistled to Basil and they cheerfully rushed down the stairs to the smart red sports car which was parked just outside the flat. They drove down the A40 in record time and arrived about half an hour later at Mr Trowel's house. Sam knocked on the door and it was opened by a young woman who told him she was Mr Trowel's housekeeper, Rosie Thomas. She led him and Basil out into the garden but seemed a little nervous as she introduced Sam to her employer.

Mr Trowel was a small man with a bald head who was about 50 years of age. He was standing by his greenhouse looking extremely cross. He told Sam that he had gone down to his greenhouse that morning and found that his prize pumpkin had disappeared, so that he could not enter it in the big competition that was being held the next day. Sam could barely hear what he was saying as loud pop music was blaring forth from the house at the bottom of his garden.

"I'll report her to the police again," he said angrily, " Gilly Gas is always playing her music too loudly."

Then he left Sam and Basil to look around the garden for clues. The detective saw it was beautifully kept; the lawn was neatly trimmed and there was a huge flower bed crammed with shrubs and colourful flowers and a vegetable plot at the bottom of the garden.

Sam spotted Mr Trowel's neighbour, a tall man staring at him over the fence, but when he went and leaned over the fence to talk there was no sign of him. He noted that the tall man also had a big vegetable patch in his garden. However he was distracted by the sound of Basil barking. When he went to see what the matter was he saw Basil had found some very large footprints in the soil that led to the gate at the bottom of the garden.

Discuss this writing

◆ Can you spot any likely suspects?
◆ Why do you think they might be suspects?
◆ What might be the reason each of them might have for taking the pumpkin?

Poem about a rainforest animal or plant

Use imagery – simile, metaphor, personification.

Choose one catchy repeating line:

Ideas:
Deep in the rainforest
Hidden in the rainforest

Animal? Tree? Plant?
Look at pictures!

Ideas: orang-utan, red-eyed tree frog, toucan, anaconda, tarantula, nibung palm tree

Simile	Compares one thing with something else using the words 'like' or 'as' *… with skin as cold as ice* *… with a beak like polished gold*
Metaphor	Compares two different things but states that something is something else *… with **white daggers** for **teeth***
Personification	Gives a human quality to something that is not human *… clinging to a lush green stem which **groans** under its weight*

Example:

Deep down in the rainforest
There is an eyelash viper
Long limbless elastic skin
Brightly coloured as yellow mustard
Inching slowly down a leaf
Like a ferocious warrior

Deep down in the rainforest…

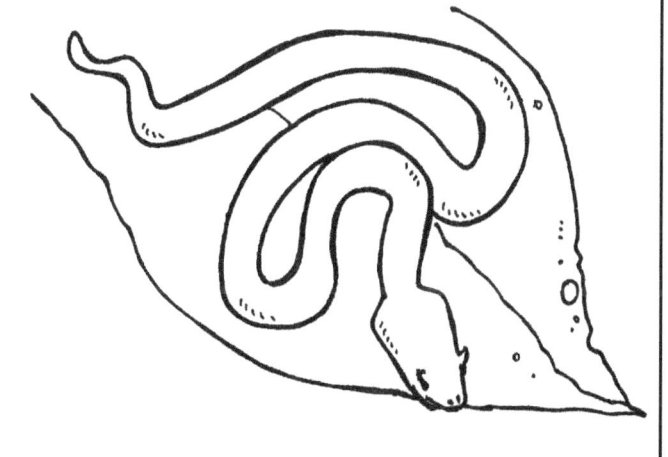

Poem about a rainforest animal or plant

Use imagery – simile, metaphor, personification.

Choose a striking part of an animal/plant/tree
Vividly compare it with something else.

fur	glowing like amber
teeth	gleaming like frosted icicles

Ideas: eyes, teeth, fur, beak, skin, bark

Movement – how?

Size – as small as…, as tall as…

Poem about a rainforest animal or plant

Use imagery – simile, metaphor, personification.

_____ (repeating line)

There is a _____

_____

_____

_____

_____

_____ (repeating line)

There is a _____

_____

_____

_____

_____

A simile poem

Similes compare one thing to another using the words 'like' or 'as'. They add description to your creative writing.

1. Visualize a picture of a pet animal, family member or yourself to describe.
2. Decide on five components that you will use and create similes to describe them.

Draft your similes on the sheet below. Have fun experimenting with them! Pick the ones you like best. (Don't forget to include some adjectives.)

Components	Ideas	Ideas
hair	Your hair is as… His hair is as… Her hair is as… My hair is as…	soft, silky, curly, spiky, brown velvet cushion, coiled spring, autumn leaf
eyes	Your eyes are like… His eyes are as Her eyes twinkle like… My eyes are as…	
ears		
legs/tail		
body		
teeth/lips		
fingers/claws		
brain		
voice/bark/purr		
smile/character trait (busy, happy, etc)		

A simile poem

By _____

Who is your poem about?
brother, dad, sister, friend, cousin, pet, me

Recurring line?
He..., She..., You..., Sister..., Me..., etc

Example:

She
Her body is as thin as a rake
She
Her hair is as curly as the rippling waves

The Battle of Hastings 1066 (a play script)

Use this information to create your play.

Cause of battle	BATTLE OF HASTINGS – 14th October 1066
In 1066 Edward the Confessor (Anglo-Saxon king of England) died. He had no children so Harold, the head of the most powerful noble family in England, was crowned king. Other people wanted the throne. Edward the Confessor's cousin William, Duke of Normandy, and the King of Norway were the main challengers. The first challenge was from the King of Norway who Harold defeated at Stamford Bridge. Then almost straight after he had to march 200 miles to Hastings to face William and his Norman army who had just arrived fresh from France . Let battle commence…..!	**Early morning** 9.00 am Harold and his army took up position at the top of a hill near Hastings and the battle with William and the Norman army began. **Midday** Normans kept charging up the hill but the English army stood strong with their shields raised. Fierce fighting but the Normans could not break through and the English army seemed to be winning. **Early afternoon** Normans tricked Saxons by pretending to retreat. Harold made a fatal mistake by ordering his army to go down the hill and chase the Normans. William ordered his army to turn round and fight. All out attack – many Saxons are hacked down. **A bit later** William ordered his archers to strike. King Harold shot in the eye and killed. Saxon army falls to pieces. William the Conqueror will now be the first Norman king of England

Think of your cast and the stage instructions and scenes.

Ideas for the cast:

Cast
Harold – King of Saxon England
William – Norman invader
Norman soldier on horse
Norman archer
Saxon foot soldier
Saxon peasant

The Battle of Hastings 1066
(a play script)

Cast:

Stage instruction(s):

Speaker	What they say

Conversations overheard

Conversations in the classroom

"Please Miss," I begged.

" No," she shouted.

"I feel ill Miss, can I go home?" I asked.

"Stop making a fuss Holly," she spluttered and her face went red with fury as she spoke.

"Can you hear them?" whispered Eliza to Sylvie.

"Nobody displeases Miss Spittlemouth," replied Sylvie.

"Holly does look a bit green, I hope she isn't sick again," mumbled Eliza.

"Have you done your history homework?" hissed Cathy from the other side of the room.

"Oh my gosh, I didn't do it – don't tell Mr Thomas," exclaimed Bella.

"The boys are going nuts next door, I am going to need help with this," begged Miss Cattelworth as she stormed into the classroom.

"I will deal with you later Holly," roared Miss Spittlemouth as she stomped out of the room.

"That will be nice," I thought sarcastically.

Conversations overheard

Write a mini-story in the form of a play script that can be acted out

Use different words for 'says' to inform the stage instructions

Ideas:
questions	laughs	groans	grasps	argues
whispers	cries	yells	sighs	grumbles
explains	chuckles	jokes	whinges	murmurs
asks	mutters	remarks	screams	criticizes

Where?
Ideas:
In the classroom
On a coach
Round the breakfast table

Cast
Names of people involved (3–4)

Idea: **The surprise letter**
Scene 1

Cast:
Lucy
Mum
Poppy
Joe

(Lucy, Mum, Poppy and Joe are all having breakfast in the kitchen)
Mum: Is that a knock on the door?
Lucy: I'll go, I'm expecting some post. *(Shouts as she hurries to the door)*
Lucy: I don't believe it! *(Whispers as she sits down again at the table)*
Poppy: What's the matter? *(Mumbles while eating her cornflakes)*
Lucy: I'm one of the winners of a short story competition organized by Radio 2. *(gasps excitedly)*
Poppy: You dark horse. I didn't know that you had the time for writing – you are always at the gym.
Lucy: Miss Jones encouraged us to send a story in the other week.
Mum: What's that you just said Lucy?
Joe: Apparently, Lucy has won a writing competition. *(Sighs Joe in a bored manner as he gets up from the table)*
Mum: Well I think that is amazing, clever girl! *(Remarks, clapping her hands)*

Boost Creative Writing, Years 5–6
© Judith Thornby and Brilliant Publications Limited

William Shakespeare – my autobiography

Facts about me
Place of birth
Birth – death
Details about my family
Marriage
Where I lived?

My career
Where did I start my acting career?
What did I write? How many?

Vocabulary:
actor   playwright   plays   histories   comedies   tragedies   sonnets

My most popular plays

Famous lines I wrote (quotes)

Important events affecting the performance of my plays

1559	Elizabeth I proclaimed travelling players could have own permanent indoor theatres
1576	James Burbidge built first theatre called The Theatre
1596	Black Death or plague rife and caused death of my son Hamnet
1597	Lease of The Theatre ran out so it was demolished. Wood from it was used to build Globe
1599	Globe theatre built
1613	Globe theatre burnt down
1614	New Globe theatre built (on same site as present-day Globe theatre)
1642	Reign of Cromwell – Puritans closed down the theatres
1660	Charles II reopened theatres/playhouses

This page may be photocopied for use by the purchasing institution only.

Boost Creative Writing, Years 5–6
© Judith Thornby and Brilliant Publications Limited

William Shakespeare – my autobiography

My autobiography

- Introduction
- Facts about me
- My plays
- Quotes
- Globe theatre
- Lord Chamberlain's Men — theatre company – Shakespeare part owner
- The theatre/playhouse
  - Why was it so popular?
  - Who were the actors?
  - Where were my plays performed?
  - What happened when the Puritans shut down the theatres?

People who came to the theatre

The Gallants
Upper class - finest clothes – wanted to be seen – posies attached to wrists to take away smell

Cutpurses
No pockets in clothes – cut purses from belts of rich – prime place to steal

Penny stinkards
Pay penny – stand in front of stage – poor – no money for soap – smelt

---

Don't forget to make it interesting!
Snappy introduction
Headings
Pictures and diagrams (label different bits)
Fun features: facts in thought bubbles, etc.

Macbeth

Write a descriptive account as if you were an observer of an encounter between three witches and two soldiers, based on the opening scenes of Macbeth.

Setting: description of the moor
Build up an atmosphere of foreboding (no characters at this stage)
What can be heard? seen? smelt?

Characters. Focus on detail (no speech yet)	
Witches	**Soldiers**
Ideas: Visual experience What are they doing? Power Pets (familiar animal spirits)	Two distant figures could be spotted crossing the moor. As they got closer it was obvious that they were… Ideas: Describe how the soldiers looked – unwashed, bloodied battle dress, etc How would they be walking and behaving after winning a long weary battle?

On first sighting the witches, how do the soldiers react?

What spells are the witches mumbling?
Make up a spell – add ingredients (eye of newt, etc).

Hubble, bubble toil and trouble
Fire burn and cauldron bubble

Macbeth

Write a descriptive account of the moor, inspired by the opening scenes of Macbeth. Build up an atmosphere of foreboding!

Setting: what could be seen on the moor?

Setting: what could be heard on the moor?

Setting: what could be smelt on the moor?

Vocabulary and useful phrases
depressing – gloomy – lonely – eerie – bleak – sinister – dark – cold – damp – foggy – grey – leaden – shadows – jagged rocks – overgrown with nettles – barren wasteland – signs of a recent battle in bloodied marsh water – thunder clap – wind howled – moaned – wailed – stink – rotting – foul – putrid – decayed

Boost Creative Writing, Years 5–6
© Judith Thornby and Brilliant Publications Limited

This page may be photocopied for use by the purchasing institution only.

Macbeth

Write a descriptive account of the three witches, inspired by the opening scenes of Macbeth.

Witch 1	
Power	
Appearance	
Pet (familiar) name – other detail	

Witch 2	
Power	
Appearance	
Pet (familiar) name – other detail	

Witch 3	
Power	
Appearance	
Pet (familiar) name – other detail	

Ideas:
Think of the witches as women, but focus on particular weird details of their appearance. Remember: their strangeness made a brave soldier like Macbeth feel uneasy.
… charcoal grey face with one normal eye and one fiery yellow snake eye…

Vocabulary and useful phrases
snake – raven – crow – bewitch the mind – guard of – massive volcano erupts when she shouts – hideous – repulsive – bearded mole

Midsummer Night's Dream

Write a descriptive account of Midsummer Night's Eve.
Somebody is astir – a very special feast is about to start. In fact, anything can happen; it is almost like a Midsummer Night's dream…

Opening sentence
It is Midsummer Night's Eve, the most magical night in the year…

Set the scene: where? who is first about? (humans are all asleep)
Use similes and bring in the senses. What can be heard, seen and smelt?

Ideas:
By a giant toadstool at the bottom of the garden
On top of a grassy hill
Deep in the woods
In amongst the mayflowers

Vocabulary:
tiptoed – fluttered – excitement – commotion

Preparations for the party
Ideas: decorations – lighting – food – music

Arrival of the guests
What do they look like? What are they wearing?

Ideas:
Mischievous elves – pixies – gnomes
Beautiful fairies with delicate wings like…
Tiny leprechaun – will o' the wisp
Majestic unicorn with a silver horn that glistened like…
Exquisite butterflies

Main event
Ideas: start of the dancing – arrival of the Fairy Queen – the Queen's speech

End of the party – reflecting on events
Maybe something is left and is found by a child in the morning…

Boost Creative Writing, Years 5–6
© Judith Thornby and Brilliant Publications Limited

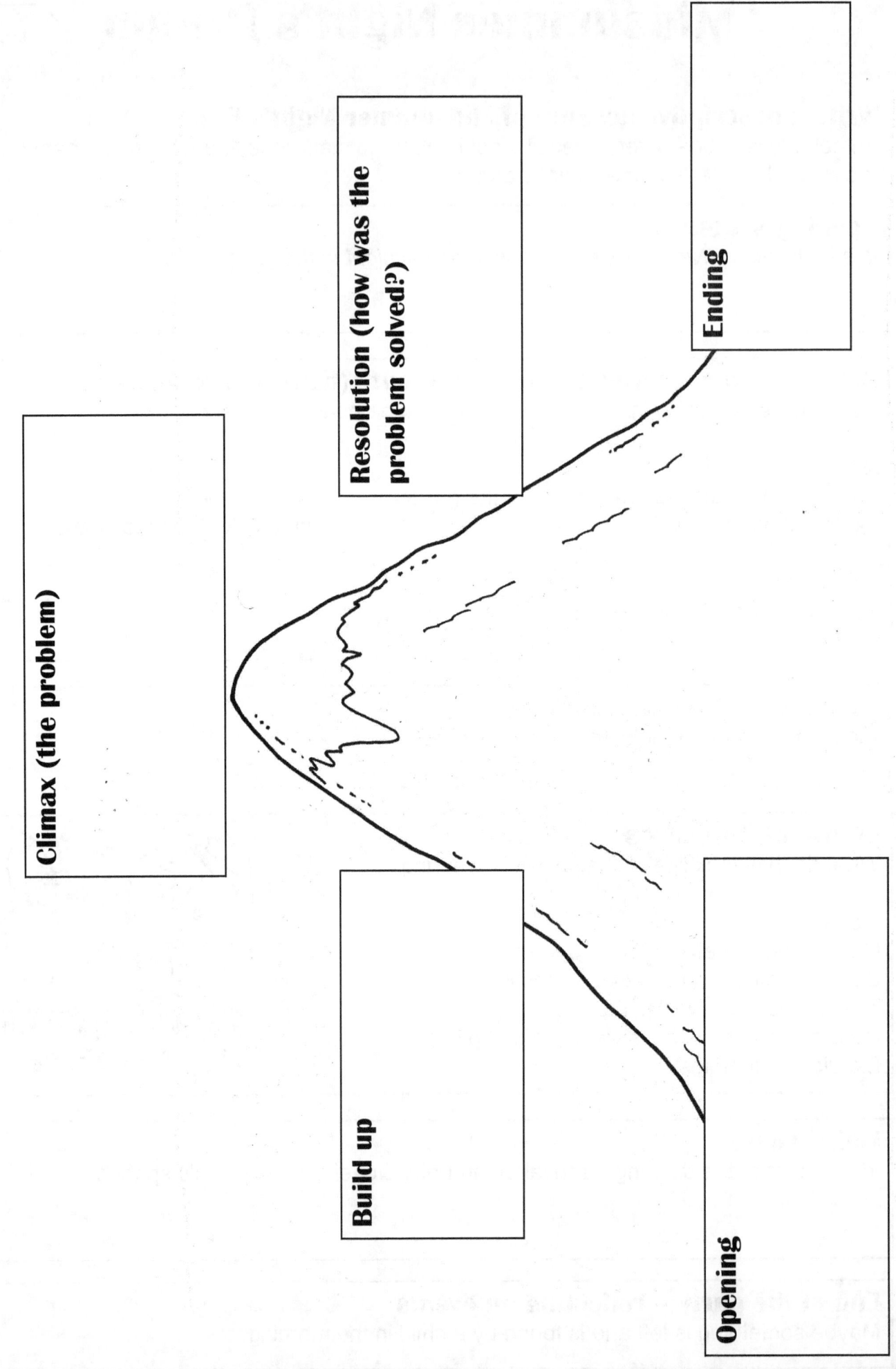

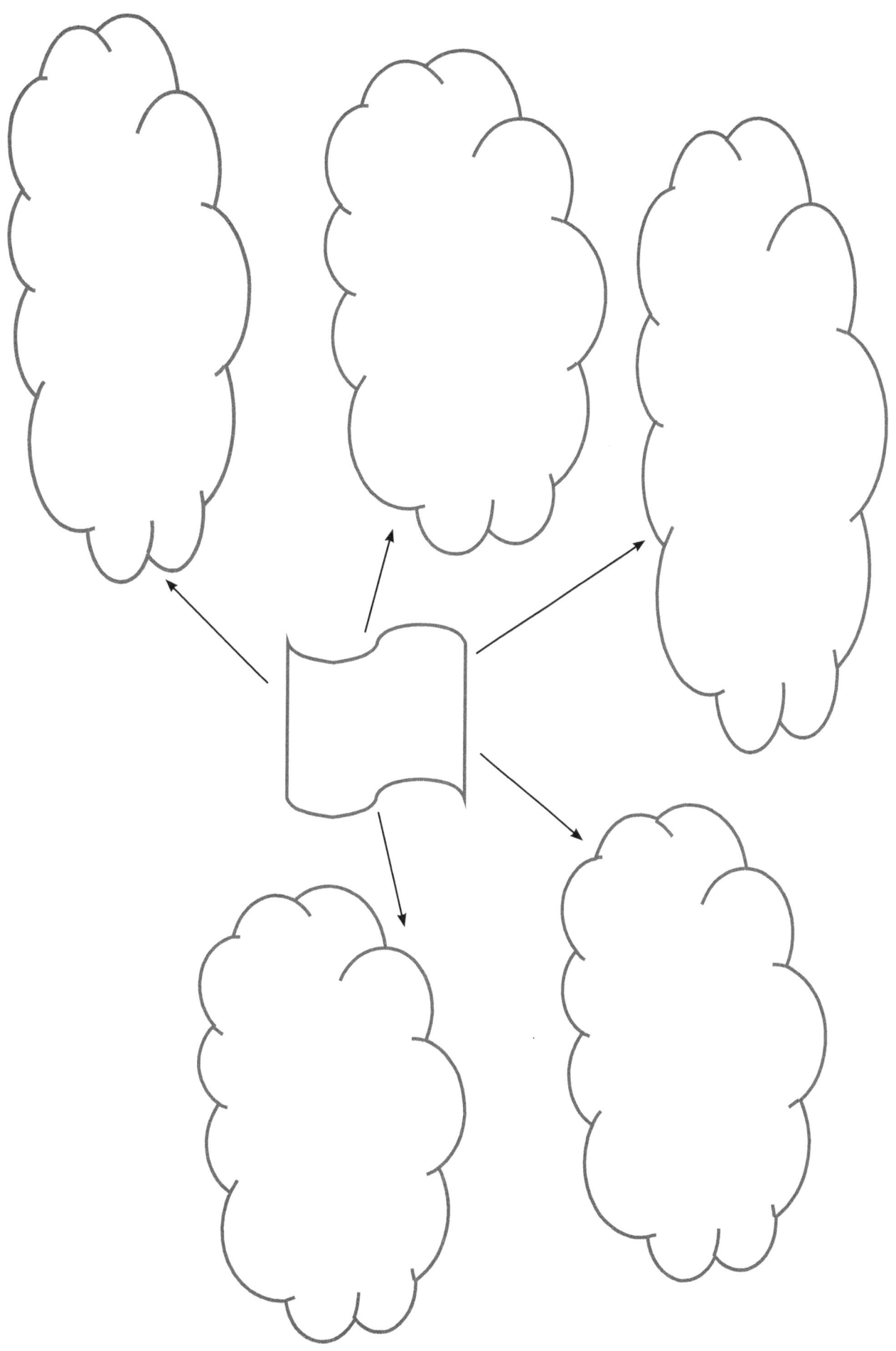

Bring in the senses

Use this sheet to use your senses when you plan your descriptive story.

Title: _____

www.ingramcontent.com/pod-product-compliance
Lightning Source LLC
Chambersburg PA
CBHW081436300426
44108CB00016BA/2379